Anonymous

Correspondence and Other Documents Relative to the

Expedition Against Tini Macomo, &c

Anonymous

Correspondence and Other Documents Relative to the Expedition Against Tini Macomo, &c

ISBN/EAN: 9783337324902

Printed in Europe, USA, Canada, Australia, Japan

Cover: Foto ©ninafisch / pixelio.de

More available books at **www.hansebooks.com**

CAPE OF GOOD HOPE.

CORRESPONDENCE

AND

OTHER DOCUMENTS

RELATIVE TO

THE EXPEDITION

AGAINST

TINI MACOMO, &c.

Printed by order of the House of Assembly.
1878.

CAPE TOWN:
SAUL SOLOMON & CO., PRINTERS, 40 & 42, ST. GEORGE'S-STREET.
1878.
[A. 52—'78.]

CAPE OF GOOD HOPE.

CORRESPONDENCE and other DOCUMENTS relative to the EXPEDITION against TINI MACOMO, &c.

𝔓rinted by order of the 𝔋ouse of 𝔄ssembly.

1878.

RETURN (in part) in compliance with a Resolution of the Honourable the House of Assembly, adopted on the 16th of July, 1878, for :—

1. All correspondence, telegraphic and other, between the Government and the Resident Magistrate of Fort Beaufort and all other persons, relative to the expedition against Tini Macomo and his brother Ngaka, including copy of Mr. Chalmers' report on his first and second visit to Tini Macomo.
2. Particulars of the charges on which the expedition was authorized, and copies of the affidavits or other documents in which they were made.
3. Return, showing the number and nature of the forces (imperial and colonial) employed in the expedition, the estimated cost thereof, the number on each side reported to have been killed or wounded, of the prisoners taken, of the cattle captured, as well as the estimated value thereof, and the appropriation of such captured cattle.
4. Copy of the instructions (if any) from Government to the Civil Commissioner of Fort Beaufort and the officers in charge of the expedition, and of the instructions from these officers to the subordinate officers of the expedition.
5. Copy of Government notice appointing a circuit court to be held at Fort Beaufort in April for trial of the prisoners taken in this expedition, with a return, showing what number (if any) were tried, with what offences charged, their respective sentences, and, if any not convicted, the grounds on which they were acquitted, and how disposed of.
6. All correspondence (if any) between the Government and Civil Commissioner of Fort Beaufort and other persons on the subject of claims or compensation for cattle or other property, alleged to have been illegally captured or damaged or destroyed.

FROM MATHEW, J. P., ADELAIDE, TO HOLLAND, C. C., FORT BEAUFORT

Mr. Campbell, the Sub-Inspector of Police, has just come from the Waterkloof, where he found the farmers in a very excited state from some information they received from a native servant, stating that Sandilli and Macomo had joined and purposed attacking them to-morrow or next day. The farmers with one exception have packed up, and purpose trekking. Mr. Campbell has used his best endeavours to persuade them to remain quiet, and on their farms, for many reasons. He has to a certain extent succeeded on condition that they be armed by the Government.

2nd December, 1877.

[A. 52—'78.]   B

TELEGRAM.

CIVIL COMMISSIONER, ALICE, TO CIVIL COMMISSIONER, FORT BEAUFORT.

Be very watchful of Gaikas; suspicious circumstance has occurred here. Let me hear any authentic information you have.

4th December, 1877.

Resident Magistrate's Office, Alice,
4th December, 1877.

Mr. Austin.

SIR,—Matters have assumed a very suspicious appearance in this neighbourhood, and I think you should be on your guard, and remove your family to some place of safety, in case of a sudden rising.

I am, &c., &c.,
(Signed)   PERCY NIGHTINGALE.

Let your neighbours know.

CIVIL COMMISSIONER, FORT BEAUFORT, TO MERRIMAN, KING WILLIAM'S TOWN.

10th December, 1877.

Reverend Van Rooy came to me to day from Tini, stating that he (Tini) had heard a rumour that he was to be apprehended and sent to Robben Island. I told him to tell Tini there was no truth in it; that the Government would protect him and his people as long as they behaved themselves. Tini also wanted to know what the volunteers were doing near his place. I told Van Rooy to tell him they were merely patrolling the district in search of thieves, as stock stealing was so much on increase. Told Van Rooy to tell him there was nothing to be afraid of, that I would be glad to see him and talk matters over ;—hoped he would render me assistance in putting a stop to thieving.

EXTRACT FROM "FORT BEAUFORT ADVOCATE," DECEMBER 28TH, 1877.

On Monday last, Tini Macomo appeared in Fort Beaufort in obedience to a summons (the second) to give evidence in a case. At the court-house there were some two hundred of his men. Why so many of them should feel interested in a paltry case it is difficult to imagine. The real object of their visit, we believe, was to give confidence to Tini (we put it mildly), who was apprehensive of his personal safety. We have also been informed by the inspector, who also furnished us with the number of Kafirs present, that the bearing of Tini and his brother was anything but respectful. Indeed it was insolent, if not defiant. The " safety of the state is the supreme law ;" we therefore applaud the action of the Governor in taking at once the steps likely to secure a large and efficient force in the present emergency. We would rather of course that His Excellency had the sanction of Parliament to back him up. We do not think it is the time to split hairs on constitutional points. As to the question of 5s. or 7s. 6d. a day to men on active duty, it is not worth considering at this moment. We have been paying double that sum to mechanics on the railways which can afford to wait; the defence of the lives and property of colonists, and the averting of a general war, if possible, is the object to be obtained. We cordially support any measures that even at this late hour may be taken by the Government to deal determinedly and effectively with the threatening danger.

3

FROM CHALMERS, FORT BEAUFORT, TO SECRETARY FOR NATIVE AFFAIRS, KING WILLIAM'S TOWN.

Have returned to this. Our movement through Stockenstrom was a very satisfactory one, and did a great deal of good. In our operations Colonel Palmer and I have throughout set our faces against any unjust act. We have dealt severely with any of our men whom we have found committing any irregularity. Fingoes who went out on their own account, and carried off cattle belonging to Kafirs, who ought not to have been interfered with, have, by our instructions, been apprehended and sent to gaol, and the cattle restored to the owners.

Cases of hardship have occurred, and which, notwithstanding all our care, could not be avoided, with some of our undisciplined forces ; but we have already satisfactorily settled some of the cases, and others are still under our investigation and consideration.

Have left Bowker and about fifty of his burghers to keep up a constant patrol from Moordenaar's kloof to Maasdorp force. This will check movement of Sandilli this way.

3rd January, 1878.

"FORT BEAUFORT ADVOCATE," JANUARY 4TH, 1878.

We hear there was a meeting at Tini Macomo's a few days ago. A councillor of Sandilli's was present. There is considerable excitement among the people, as might be expected, but there is no sign as yet of an immediate outbreak among the Gaikas there. Tini says he does not want to fight, but is afraid of attack, in the event of which his people will defend themselves. Things ought to be watched very closely in the district, in order to prevent any collision between Fingoes and Kafirs, or between Europeans and Kafirs. The latter are watchful and suspicious, and are in a temper to resist any interference with them.

It should be our plan, for the present at least, to let sleeping dogs alone.

With reference to a paragraph in our issue concerning the bearing of Tini Macomo, when here in answer to a summons to give evidence in a certain case, we find that the paragraph in question does not state exactly where Tini was insolent. On enquiring into the matter, we understand that the insolence complained of occurred outside the court-house, to inspector Booth.

"FORT BEAUFORT ADVOCATE," 11TH JANUARY, 1878.

There is nothing much to report as to Tini Macomo and his people this week, except that they are on the qui vive, and go about armed. We have been informed that a meeting has been held by his people at which a categorical demand was made as to his intentions—was it to be peace or war? He did not give a definite answer, and much dissatisfaction was created thereat. Indeed a split has occurred among them. We have heard that strange Kafirs are going into the kloofs, but we cannot vouch for the statement. A strong fort at the Blinkwater would be the thing to give confidence in that part just now. It is not true that the Kafirs in Schelmkloof are so pinched for food as some imagine. Inspector Booth informs us that he has ascertained from personal inspection that there are many corn-pits, still untouched, although food is purchased by the Kafirs.

B 2

4

Resident Magistrate's Court,
Fort Beaufort, 15th January, 1878.

Appeared before me, B. H. Holland, Esq., Resident Magistrate, Fort Beaufort, James W. Hartley, sworn states :—[*] On Saturday afternoon the 12th instant, my boy Job reported to me that he saw two strange horses running on Mr. Dreyer's farm, which he had let to natives. I told him on Sunday morning to bring the horses to me ; he returned with the horses and told me he found them tied up to a bush near to some huts, one of which is occupied by Jafta. I went up yesterday morning, in company with my son and two of my servants, to apprehend him ; on arriving there I saw him sitting against the kraal with his gun alongside of him. When Jafta saw me, he stood up and cocked his gun with the intention of shooting me, but on seeing the others come up he ran away into the bush. I told him to stand or I would fire ; he then turned round and pointed his gun at me ; just then my son fired at him. He then ran out of sight.

I subsequently sent seven men to try and apprehend him ; he snapped his gun at my son several times. Job, who saw him do this, ran round to where he was; when he got there he found Jafta pointing the gun at him. When Job saw this he fired. Jafta then ran away, leaving his gun and hat behind. I took possession of them.

(Signed)   J. W. HARTLEY.

Before me :

(Signed)   B. W. HOLLAND, Resident Magistrate.

Job, being duly sworn, states :—I am in the employ of Mr. Hartley of St. Lawrence. I reported to my master on Saturday last that there were two strange horses on Mr. Thomas Dreyer's farm, occupied by natives. On Sunday I went in search of these horses, and found them tied up to a bush. I then saw that their reims belonged to Jafta. I took these horses to my master. On Monday morning my master took two other men and myself, and went to Jafta's hut, the two others, viz : Mr. Hartley's son, Jacob, and myself, went in a different direction to Mr. Hartley. On nearing the hut I saw Jafta point the gun at my master. I then told the others who were with me, and ran towards him ; when Jafta saw us he ran away. I heard Mr. Hartley say " stand " several times. We then fired at Jafta.

I saw him point the gun at my young master ; he pulled the trigger, but the cap snapped. He also pointed the gun at me, which did not go off. I fired at the same time, and Jafta dropped his gun and ran into the bush.

I did not see him again. The gun produced is the same, both barrels were loaded, and the cap had snapped on one nipple. I know the reims belong to Jafta ; the horses don't belong to that part of the country.

(Signed)   JOB, his X mark.

Witness :—J. S. VERITY.

Before me.

(Signed)   B. W. HOLLAND, Resident Magistrate.

Fort Beaufort, 2nd February, 1878.
B. W. Holland, Esq., Civil Commissioner, Fort Beaufort.
Sir,—On behalf of Mr. George Hay, post contractor for the conveyance

[*] This is not far from Schelmkloof, and shows the feeling of the natives at this time.

5

of the mails between this town and Queen's Town, I have to request that you will firnish an escort from this town to meet the escort at Katberg, with the mails leaving at 5 a.m. to-morrow, and return as per contract time, this to continue during the present unsettled state of affairs.

(Signed) EDWARD FRISBY,
Agent for GEORGE HAY.

FROM CIVIL COMMISSIONER, FORT BEAUFORT, TO J. X. MERRIMAN, KING WILLIAM'S TOWN.

3rd February, 1878.

Yesterday Booth went to the farm of one Snodgrass adjoining Tini Macomo's to station eight men of Blakeway's police. Booth met Tini near Blinkwater Hotel; he was very insulting; he said he had not given cattle up; he was Government and would let Booth see soon. Last night Tini with one hundred armed men came to the station of Snodgrass, and ordered the police off saying he would slaughter them all if they did not leave; at the same time he threw his assegai fast in the floor. He then left; when he got to drift below the house he fired two shots; the police ran away when he first entered house, and one is missing.

Do you not think I had better now issue warrant against him for breach of the peace and theft of cattle previously reported?

FROM MERRIMAN, KING WILLIAM'S TOWN, TO CIVIL COMMISSIONER, FORT BEAUFORT.

Your course is quite clear; take out warrant on sworn affidavit of police for assault, and get a sufficient number of men to execute it, without bloodshed, if possible. You must see that you have sufficient force, which had better be led by Colonel Fry, and Blakeway must accompany as J.P. in charge. You must not let your plan leak out; and it would be desirable to defer creating a fresh centre of disturbance for a few days; meanwhile report on following points: How many men are required for the work to entirely crush resistance? What arrangements for securing rear; and what plan do you advise after consulting Blakeway?

FROM COLONEL FRY, FORT BEAUFORT, TO HONOURABLE J. X. MERRIMAN, KING WILLIAM'S TOWN.

4th February, 1878.

After lengthened conversation with Civil Commissioner, Blakeway and Booth agreed to try and surprise Tini first, failing this, force will be employed; are arranging a net work of forces, accordingly five hundred men will be required to effect his capture, one-fifth against actual resistance; remainder to be stationed at different points to cut off his retreat.

FROM MERRIMAN, KING WILLIAM'S TOWN, TO CIVIL COMMISSIONER, FORT BEAUFORT.

With reference to your telegram and Colonel Fry's, you must positively understand that no treachery, or what might be called treachery, must be used against Tini ; it always recoils on those who use it ; and do not attempt force until you are sure of success. In a few days we may most probably be able to detach force, and as I said before we don't want a fresh area of disturbance, even a small one just yet. Show this to Colonel Fry.

FROM CIVIL COMMISSIONER, FORT BEAUFORT, TO HONOURABLE J. X. MERRIMAN, KING WILLIAM'S TOWN.

No such thing as treachery ever intended. Tini is in the habit of frequenting the Blinkwater Hotel. The plan was to have a few policemen stationed there, and should he make his appearance, to apprehend him on the warrant and convoy him to Fort Beaufort.

The burgher and volunteer officers meet here to-morrow ; shall then be able to let you know the exact number of men we can bring against Tini ; should have no difficulty in crushing him were Schelmkloof not so bushy and rocky.

At Fort Beaufort on this 4th day of February, 1878, before me, Ben Herbert Holland, Resident Magistrate of Fort Beaufort, appeared James Nhlonze, who bring duly sworn, states :—I reside at Heald Town. I lost two oxen last Tuesday, one is black with white back, the other black with two white spots on sides. I traced the spoor to Blinkwater, from information received. I went this morning to shop at Blinkwater, I don't know the name. I saw the skin of my black ox with white spots, but only one spot remains, the other is cut out ; the shopkeeper told me that Ngaka brought it there. I am quite certain that it is the skin of my missing ox. Ngaka is Tini Macomo's brother.

his

(Signed)　　JAMES × NHLONZE,
mark

Witness :

J. G. VERITY,

Before me :

(Signed)　　B. H. HOLLAND,
Resident Magistrate.

4th February, 1878.

Hendrick Nel, being duly sworn, states :—I am a sergeant in Blakeway's police. On Saturday last, the first inst., Mr. Booth the sub-inspector, took me to the farm of James Snodgrass ; he stationed me with some six men. On Saturday night about 10 o'clock, Tini Macomo, with about twenty men, armed with guns and assegais, came to the house, he walked into the house, and several of his people. He said to me, "What are the police doing here?" The Fingoes replied they were there to look after people who stole. Tini said the policemen must move away from there ; he was his own policeman ; if they did not go he would slaughter them all. He rammed the assegai into the floor twice, and said, "That is the way I will slaughter you." He said, "Do you hear what I say?" He said, "I will take your guns away directly." The policemen said, "Master can do as he likes." He was violent in his manner. He said, "I am ready now, there are my guns, I am tired of this sort of thing." He flourished his assegai in a threatening manner before one of the policemen, and said, "That is the way I will serve you." He also said he would kill every policeman that came near the place, whether they had caught a thief or not. After this he left. Some of my men ran away, they were frightened ; one of them had not returned this morning. I hear that he came back to-day. Tini then left, and when he was fifty yards from the house he or his men fired off two shots.

(Signed)   H. C. NEL.

Before me.

(Signed)   B. H. HOLLAND, Resident Magistrate.

Jacob, being duly sworn, states ;—I live at Heald Town. I know the cattle of last witness. I remember his losing two oxen on Tuesday last. I saw the skin of one of the oxen at Blinkwater to-day at Walker's shop. Walker said he had bought it from Ngaka. I followed the spoor of these oxen when they were lost. I traced the spoors to Blinkwater.

(Signed)   JACOB, his X mark.

Witness :

(Signed)   J. G. VERITY.

Before me,

(Signed)   B. H. HOLLAND, Resident Magistrate.

6th February, 1878.

Samuel Walker, being duly sworn, states :—I am a shopkeeper residing at Blinkwater. I know the bullock's skin now before the court. On Monday, the 4th instant, Tini Macomo's brother brought it to my shop. I purchased it from him for 3s. 6d. The skin was afterwards claimed by a Fingo man. Tini's brother told me the skin was one of his own.

(Signed)   SAM. WALKER.

Before me,

B. H. HOLLAND, Resident Magistrate.

7th February, 1878.

James Nhlonze, being duly sworn, states :—I have just inspected the skin of the bullock produced by Mr. Walker. It is the skin of my missing ox. I know it by the white marks on the side, some of them have been cut out.

Witness :   (Signed)   JAMES NHLONZE, his X mark.

(Signed)   J. G. VERITY.

Before me,

(Signed)   B. H. HOLLAND, Resident Magistrate.

LETTER FROM REV. VAN ROOYEN.

Tidmanton, 6th February, 1878.

B. W. Holland, Esq., Civil Commissioner and Resident Magistrate,
Fort Beaufort.

SIR,—In the absence of the field-cornet of this field-cornetcy, I find it absolutely necessary in the present defenceless state we are in, and *the threatening aspect of affairs near this place*, to apply to Government through you for arms and ammunition for the following burghers who are at present on the place, and determined to stand their ground, not including the Fuller's Hoek burghers, who also belong to this field-cornetcy.

(Signed)   C. VAN ROOYEN.

FROM SPRIGG, COLONIAL SECRETARY. KING WILLIAM'S TOWN, TO CIVIL COMMISSIONER, FORT BEAUFORT.

Blakeway is to do nothing in the matter of Tini Macomo till further advised.   Let him know this.

FROM CIVIL COMMISSIONER, FORT BEAUFORT, TO HONOURABLE COLONIAL SECRETARY, KING WILLIAM'S TOWN.

8th February, 1878.

Am I to understand that Tini Macomo is not to be apprehended ? Warrants have been issued against him and his brother.   Shall Blakeway send his men back to their stations ? The Adelaide cavalry require sixty-five carbines ; can they get them at King William's Town, if an escort is sent ?

COLONIAL SECRETARY, KING WILLIAM'S TOWN, TO CIVIL COMMISSIONER, FORT BEAUFORT.

Your telegram just received gives me the first intimation of warrant having been issued against Tini and his brother.

The attempt to apprehend them must not be made.   We have so much on our hands on the frontier already that we must risk no further outbreaks at present, but bide our time ; the inhabitants of Fort Beaufort need not think that I shall fail them.   I am extremely sorry to be obliged to inform you that there is not a single gun in stock, and none are ordered from England.

FROM CIVIL COMMISSIONER, FORT BEAUFORT, TO HONOURABLE COLONIAL SECRETARY, KING WILLIAM'S TOWN.

Tini sent a message to me by native teacher, named John Sepunzi, stating that he did not turn police away, but merely asked by whose authority they were stationed on the farm of Snodgrass, as he had not been consulted.   Says he sees patrols about, and supposes it is on that account.   Sees that he has done wrong and wishes for forgiveness.   I replied that if he felt aggrieved about anything he should have come to me and I would have inquired into the matter, and he would have had justice done him. I also said he had done very wrong in going on to any one else's farm and interfering with the police; that I had reported the matter to Government; and it was for the Governor to say whether he was to be forgiven or not. Took an examination [copy examination annexed] against some Kafirs this morning for forcing their way into the house of a Winterberg farmer, named Thurtte, at night, half killing him and stealing gun, ammunition, and other articles. Have made your message to Fort Beaufort people generally known.

Fort Beaufort, 18th February, 1878.

The Honourable the Colonial Secretary, King William's Town.

With reference to the Government letter of instructions to me, No. 272 of 13th inst., I have the honour to report that, from evidence taken, it is perfectly clear that matters are in a very unsatisfactory state in the Waterkloof, and that "Tini Macomo" and his followers have been going about armed with guns and assegais, and have openly defied the police.

This state of affairs was duly reported by Mr. Holland to the Government, and that officer was instructed to take the affidavits of the police, and to issue a warrant for the apprehension of Tini Macomo for assault.

The affidavits of Sergt. Nel, and Privates James and Kondile, of Blakeway's police, were taken. These are to the effect that eight men belonging to the force were stationed by Inspector Booth on the farm of Mr. Snodgrass which adjoins Tini Macomo's farm. After dark Tini Macomo came with a number of men all armed with guns and assegais. Macomo used very threatening language to the police, stated it was war, that he would not allow the police to remain there, that if they attempted to apprehend any of his people war would be proclaimed, and that he would stab any policeman who came on his farm. His conduct and that of his followers was such that some of the policemen became frightened and ran away, and after Tini Macomo and his followers left and were about 50 yards off, they fired two shots. Mr. Booth, the inspector of native location in the Waterkloof, also reports very insolent and defiant language and conduct on the part of Tini Macomo and his followers towards himself, and that Macomo has positively refused to restore cattle, &c., which he illegally seized from some natives.

Upon these affidavits Mr. Holland issued a warrant for the apprehension of Tini Macomo, charging him with public violence and riot, and assault or breach of the peace. Plans were made to apprehend Macomo. The Kafirs, however, became acquainted with the plans and intentions regarding Macomo, and thereupon the Kafirs from Adelaide and surrounding country flocked towards Macomo's location, their intention being to resist any attempt to apprehend him.

The warrant was not put into execution, nor was there any attempt made to do so. There was, therefore, no resistance offered to its execution, but it is perfectly clear that resistance was intended.

Before any steps were taken to execute the warrant Mr. Holland received the following telegram from Government:—"The attempt to apprehend Tini Macomo and his brother must not be made. We have so much on our hands on the frontier already that we must risk no further outbreaks at present, but bide our time ⚬ ⚬ ⚬."

Nothing further, therefore, has been done in the matter. There is also a warrant issued against Tini Macomo's brother, " Ngaka," for theft, but no attempt has been made to execute it. Tini and his immediate followers sleep in the Schelmkloof bush.

I may here state that the Honourable Mr. Ayliff mentioned to me in King William's Town that there was a case of theft pending against Tini Macomo, and that he could at any time be apprehended on that charge. I have looked into the case. I find that Macomo seized stock and firearms from Kafirs who were tried for theft and convicted ; that he still retains these, and refuses to restore them. On the record, however, the Solicitor-General gives his opinion that he " does not think a jury would find Tini Macomo guilty of theft, and that the parties aggrieved had better be left to their civil remedy." And the late Attorney-General, Mr. Stockenstrom, gives the following opinion on the case :—" The Solicitor-General was quite right in the view taken by him of the law. Tini Macomo did not take the articles in question as a thief, but openly, and by virtue of an imaginary claim. I think, at the same time, that steps should be taken by Government to make Macomo understand that he does not possess any power as a chief." Macomo has defied the magistrate of the district, and refuses to restore the articles to the owners.

I take the liberty of remarking that the sooner men like Tini Macomo are taught that they cannot interfere with, or seize the property of others, the better will it be for the peace of the Colony and the credit of our Government.

Besides all these matters farmers have for a long time past been suffering a great deal from the thefts committed by the Kafirs in the Waterkloof. These Kafirs have turned out in armed bodies to prevent farmers following up and recovering their property. A very severe assault has lately been committed by Kafirs on a farmer, and altogether the state of insecurity in this district, arising from the lawless and rebellious attitude of the Kafirs, is such that nearly all the farmers have left their farms.

There is no doubt that the employment of Fingoes against the Kafirs is most irritating to the Kafirs, and that a great deal of mischief is thus created where mischief would not otherwise arise. But when the Government sees fit to employ Fingoes as policemen under European officers I submit that it becomes the imperative duty of the Government to protect them and uphold their authority, and to allow no excuse for Kafirs turning out armed to resist them or to interfere with them.

I have endeavoured to lay before the Government, as clearly as possible, the true state of affairs. I am of opinion that Tini Macomo and his followers who turned out armed, and who interfered with, and used threatening language, towards Sergeant Nel and the police, and towards Superintendent Booth (men who have been duly appointed by the Government) have committed an offence for which they ought to be apprehended and punished ; and that they as well as others should be taught that such lawless and rebellious conduct will not be tolerated in the colony.

Tini Macomo has sent in a message to Mr. Holland asking forgiveness, but I submit that it would show great weakness on our part if his conduct were allowed to go unpunished.

It will now be for the Government to decide what course is to be adopted in the matter. If it is determined to apprehend Tini Macomo there is no doubt that resistance will be offered. From information received from reliable men I find that from 800 to 1,000 men would rally round him. It will therefore be necessary to have a strong force to carry out the intentions of the Government, and the longer we put off decided action the worse will matters become in the Waterkloof, and I submit that it becomes highly necessary to clear those fastnesses of Kafirs, and on no account allow them to occupy them in future. It was a great mistake allowing the Gaikas again to come in possession of the Waterkloof, and I think the

Government should purchase the land and give it out in lots to Scotch or German immigrants.

Action may be commenced by Mr. Holland being instructed to send to Macomo and his brothers calling upon them to appear before him on a stated day to answer the charge of turning out armed with his followers and interfering with the police and the superintendent, or otherwise abide the consequences.

(Signed.)   W. B. CHALMERS.

Fort Fordyce, 18th February, 1878.

C. F. Blakeway, Esq., Inspector District Police, Fort Beaufort.

Sir,—I have the honour to report for your information that a party of police were sent on Saturday on the spoor of stolen sheep. They report having traced them on to Macomo's farm, near some huts. The Kafirs obstructed them in their duty, and threatened their lives should they again come on Macomo's ground. Our party is not strong enough to carry out the law in Schelmkloof and Blinkwater. I think it would be better for the *present* not to send men down, as we only make things worse, not being able to perform our duty owing to the disaffected state of the natives, and the small party of men at my command. I also beg to report three of the police for deserting their party, when they apprehended danger, and thereby weakening the party, their names are Christian, Charles, and Thychobeni.

I have, &c.,

(Signed)   A. G. CAMPBELL,
Sub-Inspector, D.P.

A true copy : W. B. CHALMERS, 18th February, 1878.

FROM COLONIAL SECRETARY, KING WILLIAM'S TOWN, TO CIVIL COMMISSIONER, FORT BEAUFORT.

Lay whole case of Tini before Chalmers, who has power to act.

At Fort Beaufort, on the 18th day of February, 1878, before me, Ben Herbert Holland, Resident Magistrate for Fort Beaufort, appeared Margan, who, being duly sworn, states :—On Saturday last, the 16th instant, I was acting corporal in Mr. Blakeway's police. I was stationed at Fort Fordyce with eleven men under Sergeant Heagan. Jacob Ntshuntshe, *alias* Baleni, reported to Heagan that he had lost nine sheep. Heagan sent me with nine men to look for them. We found the spoor between Fort Fordyce and Tini's place ; we followed the spoor to near Tini's location ; we then lost it. A man from Tini came to us ; we were on his ground ; asked us what we wanted there ; we said we were tracing a spoor. He said, " Who told you to come on to Tini's ground ?" We said " We did not know there was any barrier ; we thought we had the right to follow a spoor anywhere." he asked whose sheep we were looking for. We said Baleni's. This man said Baleni knows he has no right here. While he was still talking some other men came from Tini's with guns and assegais. There were more than forty ; they all asked us what we wanted. They said the magistrate or Government could not send a policeman on to Tini's ground ; they said they were tired of us always coming that way ; they were waiting for us ; they said the next policeman they caught on that farm they would kill him. They

c 2

surrounded us, and kept us there from midday till near sunset. They would not let us go ; I would know them again ; I know them to be Tini's people ; when they put their assegais to our faces one of them had a breech loader, some had double barrelled muzzle loaders, and others muskets, I don't think there were more than ten guns.

(Signed)   MARGAN,   his × mark.

Witness :

(Signed)   J. G. VERITY.

Before me :

(Signed)   B. H. HOLLAND,
Resident Magistrate.

STATEMENT OF THOMAS CLARKE, CHIEF CONSTABLE, FORT BEAUFORT.

On Saturday, 23rd February last, I proceeded to Schelmkloof with a summons and two subpœnas in a case of rescue of cattle. The plaintiff promised to meet me at Mr. Snodgrass' house, and go with me to point out the parties, but he did not do so, and I was obliged to engage a Kafir named Nauto, who resides on Mr. Snodgrass' farm, who told me that he knew the parties. Myself, Nauto, and my son Walter, proceeded together to Mr. Sweetnam's farm, Sittingbourne, where we found the defendant. I then served him with the summons personally ; the two subpœnas were for persons residing about a mile higher up the kloof. Mr. Sweetnam and his volunteers who were resting on his farm, informed me that they had been to the place where I was going, and that the Kafirs of those kraals were now in the bush, and that it was unsafe for me to go there alone. I then gave the subpœnas to Nauto to serve upon the wives, if the men were not there. On Nauto's return he informed me that as he was proceeding with the subpœnas, two Kafirs came suddenly upon him, out of the bush, and stopped him. One was armed with a gun and the other with assegais. They questioned him and asked him if he was not a policeman, and after detaining him for some time, allowed him to go on, telling him at the same time that the men were not there. He said that he saw several Kafirs watching Sweetnam's party from the bush.

(Signed)   THOMAS CLARKE,
Chief Constable, Fort Beaufort.

Tuever Fontein, March 2nd, 1878.

C. P. Owen, who being duly sworn, states :—I am a farmer residing on the farm Rietvley, in the field-cornetcy of Winterberg, in the division of Fort Beaufort. Coming from Fort Beaufort on Wednesday last, I left a knocked-up ox in charge of two Kafirs living at a kraal on Mr. Shaw's farm—the second kraal below the outspan. I went for the ox on Tuesday the 26th last month, and got the ox at the kraal. Whilst I was there a Kafir named Jafta, living on the same farm, brought a note from Mr. Shaw, which he took out of his pocket. He gave the note to me to read. It was a printed form for rent, with the amount not filled in, and the name of the farm Lequard. It was written on the other side—the writing of which I could not read. I believe it was in Kafir; there was no signature nor date to the paper; there was an address on the envelope, and a postage stamp. Jafta only gave me the enclosed, and kept the envelope.

I handed Jafta the note back again, and told him I could not understand it, and then a conversation took place between the Kafirs, "Jafta" being the principal spokesman. He spoke very fast. I could not catch anything that was said. When he had done, the other man then laughed, and said in English, "Oh, they are ready." This man read the printed form, and then he called me on one side. He said to me, "Baas, if you don't want to be in the war, you must go home at once and pack up your wagon. If you don't want to go away send your wife and children away. If you come here with your wagon we will take you through as far as Baker's." I asked him " why ?" He said " because Mr. Shaw has sent us word that we must pay the rent this week. If we have not got money enough we must bring our cattle into Fort Beaufort and sell them, because they (meaning Government) are going to attack us next week." I then put the question, " Who do you mean by they ?" He said " The soldiers ; the Government." I said the soldiers were coming to Fordyce, and to be stationed about to prevent stealing. He said the police and Sweetnam's volunteers could not stop thieving. How could they stop it? There were about a dozen men at the huts, two guns, and a number of assegais. He particularly called my attention to the arms ; he said they intended to fight.

(Signed)   C. P. OWEN.

Sworn before me in the presence of the subscribing witnesses on the above date.

(Signed)   J. SWEETNAM, Justice of the Peace.

Witnesses :

C. F. SWEETNAM,
W. HOOLE.

WARRANT OF APPREHENSION.

To the Field-cornets, Constables, Police Officers, and other Officers of the Law proper to the execution of Criminal Warrants.

Whereas from information taken upon oath before me, there are reasonable grounds of suspicion against Ngaka of Blinkwater, that he did on the 29th day of January, 1878, commit the crime of Theft.

These are, therefore, in Her Majesty's name, to command you that immediately upon sight hereof you apprehend and bring the said Ngaka, or cause him to be apprehended and brought before me to be examined, and to answer to the said information and to be further dealt with according to law.

Given under my hand at Fort Beaufort this 8th day of February, 1878.

(Signed)   B. H. HOLLAND,
Resident Magistrate.

Mortally wounded in action on or about the 8th March, 1878, at Sweetnam's Kloof.

(Signed)   B. H. HOLLAND,
Resident Magistrate.

WARRANT OF APPREHENSION.

Ben Herbert Holland, Esq., Resident Magistrate for the District of
Fort Beaufort.

*To the Field-cornets, Constables, Police Officers, and other Officers of the Law
proper to the execution of Criminal Warrants.*

Whereas, from information taken upon oath before me, there are
reasonable grounds of suspicion against Tini Macomo of Blinkwater, that
he did on the 2nd and 16th day of February, 1878, commit the crime of
sedition.

These are, therefore, in Her Majesty's name, to command you that
immediately upon sight hereof you apprehend and bring the said Tini
Macomo, or cause him to be apprehended and brought before me to be
examined, and to answer to the said information, and to be further dealt
with according to law.

Given under my hand at Fort Beaufort, this 20th day of February, 1878.

(Signed)   B. H. HOLLAND,
Resident Magistrate.

STATEMENT OF THOMAS CLARKE, CHIEF CONSTABLE, FORT BEAUFORT.

On Saturday, the 2nd March, 1878, I proceeded, in company with my
son, Frederick William, and a Kafir named Maholo, to Schelmkloof, for the
purpose of executing a writ of attachment on a judgment of this court in
the case of *Maholo* versus *Sam*. On arriving at Mr. Snodgrass' farm, the
plaintiff informed me that the defendant "Sam" had removed to a kraal
on Tini Macomo's farm. I went there and saw the defendant, and after
explaining to him the service upon which I was sent I demanded the
amount of the debt and costs, which was about £8. He said that he had no
money. I told him that I would have to take two head of cattle, which he
could release within fourteen days upon paying the debt and costs. He refused
to point out his cattle. The plaintiff "Maholo" then pointed them out to me.
I took possession of one ox and one cow. He got into a violent passion, and
said that if I took his cattle I would have to take him also. I remonstrated
with him, and endeavoured to pacify him by explaining the law to him. He
then got quite outrageous, and one of his sons endeavoured to rescue the
cattle, which were then under charge of my son. I handed the cattle
over to Maholo to drive to Fort Beaufort. Maholo had got about 100 yards
from the kraal when six men armed with knobkerries ran after him and
commenced assaulting him. I drew my revolvers, and I and my son ran
to his assistance. We rescued him. These men accused him of theft, and we
had great difficulty in preventing them from assaulting him again. I
started him off again with the cattle, and I remained at the kraal until he
was a considerable distance on the road, and then followed him to Fort
Beaufort. There were a great many Kafirs about the place quietly looking
on, and had I attempted to arrest any of these men, I have no doubt we
would have had the whole of the Kafirs of the location up in arms against
us, as the demeanour of these six men and the defendant towards both
me and my son was very insulting. I don't know the names of any of
the men; they were all strangers to me.

(Signed)   T. CLARKE, Chief Constable.

15

Resident Magistrate's Court,
Fort Beaufort, 18th February, 1878.

Before me, Ben Herbert Holland, Esquire, Resident Magistrate for Fort Beaufort, in presence and hearing of William and Junga, charged with the crime of theft, appeared.

Gert Nel, who being duly sworn, states :—I am a farmer residing at Kaal Hoek. On Friday, the 15th instant, I lost sixty-eight sheep. On Saturday morning I found the spoors, and the spoors of two men following the sheep. I traced the spoor from my place to Schelmkloof. We returned home on Saturday night, and went back to take up the spoor on Sunday morning. We found where the sheep had been slaughtered ; we found 46 skins and heads. My mark was on the ears of the sheep. They were also marked with the letter G. on the skin. It was not far from the kraal of the prisoners. We traced a number of spoors from this spot to the huts of the prisoners. We searched their huts, but found nothing. We found the carcases of fifteen sheep hanging up in trees about 600 yards from prisoner's huts. Two people ran away when we came near the kraal of the prisoners.

Cross-examined by Tunga :—You were near the kraal with cattle.
William declines to cross-examine.

(Signed)   G. NEL.

Before me,

(Signed)   B. H. HOLLAND,
Resident Magistrate.

———

Thomas Dreyer, being duly sworn, states :—I live at Kaal Hoek. On Saturday at 12 o'clock Nel reported to me that he had lost some sheep. I and four other people accompanied him. We took the spoor from near his place to the other side Mr. Croft's house. It got dark, and I returned to the laager. Yesterday morning I took the spoor up again from this spot and traced it close to Schelmkloof where I found the slaughter place I counted forty-six skins, and a good many heads. The skins had Mr. Nel's mark, and also the ears. Several of the skins are now before the court. They are so decomposed, it is difficult to distinguish the mark, but there was no doubt about it when I first saw them. I found a great number of spoors where the sheep had been slaughtered. It had been raining and the spoors were easily distinguishable. I sent for the police, which were at Snodgrasss' farm, and Captain Edwards, with ten men, came from Post Retief. When they arrived we traced the spoors from the spot to the huts where prisoners live. We traced it between the huts. We saw prisoner William standing on a krantz, evidently on the watch. We traced the spoor close by where he was standing to his kraal. Edwards and I, in company with two men, then went back, and Edwards came out close to prisoner William. He ran away. Edwards told him to stand or he would shoot him. He stood. We apprehended him and took four of his assegais from him. We went to the huts ; there are ten or twelve, but all the people had left with the exception of four old women and four young children. We saw some natives standing at the edge of the bush about two hundred yards off. I sent some of the men round to try and catch them. When my men came in sight they called upon them to stand. They ran away and two shots were fired at them. This was one of the kloofs that run out of Schelmkloof. The kraal is on Mr. Shaw's ground.

The Kafirs after this shouted from the bush in Dutch, *if we wished to make war they were ready.* The prisoner Tuga was found hiding away in a little bush near the kraal. We did not like going into the kloof, as we thought they were too many for us.

Cross-examined by William :—There were no cattle near you.

Tunga declines to cross-examine.

(Signed)   T. F. DREYER.

Before me :

(Signed)   B. H. HOLLAND,
Resident Magistrate.

Copy.]

Prisoner's Name and Description.	Crime.	Date of Apprehension, if apprehended—if not, state that not in custody.	Whether committed for Trial or for further Examination, Committing Magistrate's Name, Date of Committal, and Prison to which committed.	Whether Bail found or not.	Remarks and Instruction of the Attorney-General.
Jan Kalife—Kafir—30 years	Assault with intent to do some grievous bodily harm.	11th February, 1878.	Committed for trial by B. H. Holland, Resident Magistrate for Fort Beaufort, on this, the 13th of February, 1878, to the Fort Beaufort gaol.	Not.	
William Magali—Kafir—40 years					
Jan Martinus—Kafir—30 years					

15th February, 1876.

(Signed)   B. H. HOLLAND, Resident Magistrate.

[A. 52—'78.]   D

Resident Magistrate's Court,
Fort Beaufort, 14th February, 1878.

Before me, B. H. Holland, Resident Magistrate for the said district, and in the presence and hearing of prisoners.

Jan Kalife, William Magali, Jan Martinus, Jan Puzani, and January, now in their sound and sober senses, charged with assault with intent to do some grievous bodily harm and theft, appeared.

Edward Goddard Thurlte, who, being duly sworn, states :—I am a farmer residing at Cypherfontein in this district. On Sunday night, the 10th instant, after I had retired to rest, I heard knocking at my door. I got up, struck a light, lit the candle and opened the door. I saw William Magali. He said he had a note for me. Just as I put my hand out for it, he seized me round the neck and forced me against the wall. I called to my wife to shoot them. The gun was on the bed. Jan Martinus then seized me by the throat. William Magali then got hold of my gun and handed it to some others outside. Some of them then dragged my wife out of bed and led her outside. I was nearly fainting from the pressure on my throat, when one of them pulled my legs from under me. I fell, and Jan Martinus knelt on my stomach. William then asked me where my double barrel gun was. I told him it was gone. He said I lied. They said they would not kill me if I would give them the gun. Jan Martinus then rushed across and struck me with his fist in the eye. They also pulled a quantity of my beard out. They after this threw me on the ground again, and strangled me to such an extent that I lost consciousness. When I came round, I found Jan Kafili leaning over me. I can only swear to the three men. My wife went down to call the Hottentots, who live about forty yards from the house. I afterwards followed her, and whilst there Jan Kafili came, and said I must come with my gun as people were stealing Mr. Ogilvie's sheep. I took my horse and rode down to Post Retief for assistance. They stole my carbine, gunbucket, 30 rounds of snider ammunition, one knife, two pocket-knives, two pipes, and some tobacco, a shawl and some bread, meat and corn, saddle, saddlecloth and bridle, purse containing about £2 5s., powder flask, half pound gun-powder, padlock and key, pair of earrings. William Magali said it was little Kreli's work this, but the big business was coming.

Cross-examined by Mr. De Wet :—This all happened inside the house. I have known all the prisoners for some time. I have always been on good terms with them. On Sunday a horse of mine had gone into the lands of William Magali. He made a noise about it. None of the articles have been recovered.

(Signed)   EDWARD THURTELL.

Before me :

(Signed)   B. H. HOLLAND,
Resident Magistrate.

—— ——

Sophia Thurtell, being duly sworn, states :—I am the wife of last witness. I remember hearing a knock at our door on Sunday night last. My husband lit a candle and went to the door and opened it. I saw William Magali at the door ; he said had brought a note. My husband asked him for it. He immediately caught my husband by the throat, and Jan Martinus then jumped and also caught him by the throat. Two more came in. They threw my husband down. Jan Martinus then pulled me out of bed, and Willem took the gun away from me. Jan Martinus took me outside, and told me if I spoke he would shoot me. I can only identify the two I have mentioned. One of those outside called out, saying that those inside were to cut my husband's throat, but another said "do not do it." I saw five there. All I saw taken was the saddle, pouch, and gun.

Prisoners decline cross-examining.

her
SOPHIA × THURTELL.
mark

Witnesses :

(Signed)   A. HUDSON.
             J. G. VERITY.

Before me :

(Signed)   B. H. HOLLAND,
             Resident Magistrate.

15th February, 1878.

Henry Rowland Palmer, being duly sworn, states :—I am district surgeon. Yesterday I examined a man named Edward Goddard Thurtell. He had a severe contusion of the right eye, several bruises over the right eye-brow and forehead on that side, marks of violence about his throat on both sides and the middle, such as would be caused by human finger nails ; also swelling under the right ear, considerable abrasion of the skin from the right shoulder blade. He complained of great pain and tenderness over the breast bone over the region of the liver and stomach, and also across the back the pain or tenderness over the front of his body was very much increased by the least pressure. He informed me that he vomited some blood after the receipt of the injuries. He was under considerable degree of nervous excitement when I saw him, arising from the injuries, and I have no doubt he is suffering from several internal bruises. These injuries must have been caused by violent pressure. Those on the face by blows from a fist, with the exception of the one on the forehead, which was probably caused by a fall. The marks on the throat were caused by pressure from human fingers. This must have been severe, as the skin was lacerated in several places by nails.

Cross-examined by Mr. De Wet :—I do not consider Thurtell in any danger of his life. He will probably be all right in a few weeks.

(Signed)   H. R. PALMER.

Before me :

(Signed)   B. H. HOLLAND,
             Resident Magistrate.

18th February, 1878.

In presence and hearing of Jan Kalife, William Magali and Jan Martinus, charged with the crime of assault with intent to do some grievous bodily harm.

Appeared, Thomas Schmidt, who, being duly sworn, states :—I am a farmer residing at Kaal Hoek. On the Monday after Thurtell was assaulted, Jan Kalife came to where I am at present with my oxen. He had two assegais in his hand. Barend Botha was with me. He asked him what was the matter. He replied Thurtell is murdered. I don't understand Kafir, but Botha interpreted for me. He also said that the sheep he looked after (Ogilvie's) had got out of the kraal, and a number were away, and he said six Kafirs had come to him and told him to go and tell Thurtell that Kreli was here, and when he went to Thurtell he found he had fainted. He remained there a short time, and Thurtell came to his senses. He said they had taken two guns and ammunition from Thurtell and his saddle, and said Thurtell had gone to to Sweetnam's.

Prisoners decline cross-examination.

(Signed)   T. SCHMIDT.

Before me :

(Signed)   B. H. HOLLAND,
Resident Magistrate.

Copy.]

PRELIMINARY EXAMINATION.

In the case of the Queen *versus* Jan Kalife, charged with assault with intent to do some grievous bodily harm and theft.

District of Beaufort.

At Fort Beaufort, in the district of Fort Beaufort, on the 15th day of February, 1878, in the presence of Ben Herbert Holland, Resident Magistrate for the said district, appeared Jan Kalife, 26 years of age, born at by trade or occupation, labourer, residing at Winterberg, who, having heard the evidence adduced in support of the charge made against him, of having on the 10th day of February, 1878, and at Cypherfontein, in the district of Fort Beaufort, commited the crime of assault with intent to do some grievous bodily harm and theft, and being asked what he will say in answer thereto, and being at the same time cautioned that he is not obliged to make any statement that may criminate him, and that what he shall say may be used in evidence against him, declares, I know othing.

his
(Signed)   JAN × KALIFE
mark.

The above declaration was freely and voluntarily made by the said Jan Kalife, who was then in his sound and sober senses, and having been read over and interpreted to him, adhered to the same, and affixed his mark thereto in the presence of the subscribed witnesses, and

Before me :

(Signed)   B. H. HOLLAND,
Resident Magistrate.

Witnesses :

(Signed)   W. A. HUDSON,
(Signed)   J. G. VERITY.

Copy.]

PRELIMINARY EXAMINATION.

In the case of the Queen *versus* William Magali, charged with assault with intent to do some grievous bodily harm and theft.

District of Beaufort.

At Fort Beaufort, in the district of Fort Beaufort, on the 15th day of February, 1878, in the presence of Ben Herbert Holland, Resident Magistrate for the said district, appeared William Magali, 40 years of age, born at   , by trade or occupation, labourer, residing at Winterberg, who, having heard the evidence adduced in support of the charge made against him of having on the 10th day of February, 1878, and at Cypherfontein, in the district of Fort Beaufort, committed the crimes of assault with intent to do some grievous bodily harm and theft, and being asked what he will say in answer thereto, and being at the same time cautioned that he is not obliged to make any statement that may criminate him, and that what he shall say may be used in evidence against him, declares, I know nothing.

his
(Signed)   WILLIAM × MAGALI.
mark.

The above declaration was freely and voluntarily made by the said William Magali, who was then in his sound and sober senses, and having been read over and interpreted to him, adhered to the same, and affixed his mark thereto, in the presence of the subscribing witnesses, and

Before me :
(Signed)   B. H. HOLLAND,
Resident Magistrate.

Witnesses :
(Signed)   W. H. Hudson,
J. G. Verity.

PRELIMINARY EXAMINATION.

In the case of the Queen *versus* Jan Martinus, charged with assault with intent to do some grievous bodily harm, and theft.
District of Beaufort.

At Fort Beaufort, in the district of Fort Beaufort, on the 15th day of February, 1878, in the presence of Ben Herbert Holland, Resident Magistrate for the said district, appeared Jan Martinus, 35 years of age, born at ———, by trade or occupation, labourer, residing at Winterberg, who, having heard the evidence adduced in support of the charge made against him of having, on the 10th day of February, 1878, and at Cypherfontein, in the district of Fort Beaufort, committed the crime of assault with the intent to do some grievous bodily harm and theft, and being asked what he will say in answer thereto, and being at the same time cautioned that he is not obliged to make any statement that may criminate himself, and that what he shall say may be used in evidence against him, declares, I know nothing.

his
JAN × MARTINUS.
mark.

The above declaration was freely and voluntarily made by the said Jan Martinus, who was then in his sound and sober senses, and having been read over and interpreted to him, adhered to the same, and affixed his mark thereto in the presence of the subscribing witnesses, and

Before me :
(Signed)   B. H. HOLLAND,
Resident Magistrate.

Witnesses :
(Signed)   A. Hudson,
J. G. Verity.

MR. CHALMERS, SPECIAL COMMISSIONER, FORT BEAUFORT, TO COLONIAL SECRETARY, KING WILLIAM'S TOWN.

19th February, 1878.

Tini Macomo and his followers have been going about armed with guns and assegais, and been defying the police. Eight men under a European officer, belonging to Blakeway's police, were stationed on a farm adjoining Macomo's. After dark Macomo, with a number of men all armed with guns and assegais, came and used threatening language to the police. Macomo stated it was war; that he would not allow police to remain there; that if they attempted to apprehend any of his people war would be proclaimed; that he would stab any policeman who came on his farm. His conduct and that of his followers was such that some of the policemen became frightened and ran away. Two shots were fired by Macomo's men. Their language and demeanour has also been very insulting to Inspector Booth. Macomo has positively refused to carry out the magistrate's orders to give up stock and firearms, which he illegally seized from certain farmers. Government issued orders to Mr. Holland to take out a warrant for the apprehension of Macomo. Before it was put into execution it was counter ordered by the Government. The Kafirs, however, heard of it, and they flocked from Adelaide and surrounding country to Macomo's place, with the intention of resisting his apprehension. There is also a warrant out against Tini's brother for theft. The amount of stealing that is carried on by the Kafirs in the Waterkloof is something frightful. The Kafirs turn out in armed parties to prevent farmers following up and recovering their property. A very severe assault had been committed by Kafirs on a farmer, and altogether the state of insecurity in this district, arising from the lawless and rebellious attitude of the Kafirs, is such that nearly all the farmers have left their farms. Macomo sent in a messenger to Holland, asking forgiveness for his conduct; but I submit that he has gone too far, and that it would now show great weakness on our part to overlook the conduct of himself and followers. It was a sad mistake allowing Kafirs again to get into the Waterkloof, and I think we ought now to take chance of clearing them out. Macomo and his followers sleep in the Schelmkloof Bush.

FROM MATHEW, J. P., ADELAIDE, TO CIVIL COMMISSIONER, FORT BEAUFORT.

Have given Campbell his directions. Van Vuren reports to me this morning as follows:—On Saturday night the Kafirs stole four of my oxen. I followed spoor down bush neck, and out of Gilbert's kloof, down to Schelmkloof. I had with me five Europeans and eight Fingo police. About forty yards from Schelmkloof I was accosted by a Kafir named Suel. He asked me how dare I come on his ground. I told him I was seeking my stolen cattle. With Suel were thirty natives armed with guns and assegais. This number gradually increased to one hundred and fifty. Finding my party too weak to enter the kloof, I offered Suel thirty shillings to assist me with ten of his men and two of the Fingo police. My cattle were brought out. I wish you would inform the Magistrate that there are so many armed natives.

Fort Beaufort, 11th January, 1878.

Gwanya, being duly sworn, states:—I am a Gaika Kafir, residing at Blinkwater. I live on Tini Macomo's farm. I was to pay him when I reaped my crops. I have been there a year. I live with my brother, and he paid Tini a cow. I know that a man named Mama had two oxen stolen from him ; the head and the meat were found at the kraal where I live. I was apprehended on the charge of being concerned in the theft, and released while I was in gaol. I had one gun and a heifer taken from my place. My brother's wife Ziti told me this after I was released, and I found the things missing when I returned home. I went to see Tini about it. I asked him for my gun and heifer. He said you will not get them as you are a thief. I saw the gun in Tini's hut, and my heifer in his kraal. Tini keeps them because he says I gave his farm a bad name. These things were taken on the 24th December, 1877.

his

(Signed) GWANYA ×

mark.

Before me :

(Signed) B. H. HOLLAND,

Resident Magistrate.

Witnesses :

    (Signed) W. A. HUDSON,
            J. G. VERITY.

    Ziti, sworn, states :--I am married to the last witness's nephew. I live at the same kraal. I remember the beads and skins of stolen cattle being found near the huts. I remember Tini coming to our huts the day after Christmas. He took a gun out of the hut of last witness. I know the gun belongs to him (last witness). Tini also took a heifer belonging to the last witness. He said he was taking them because we had given his place a bad name. He also took six head of cattle, the property of of Booy, now a prisoner in the gaol. I know the cattle belong to Booy. He also took a gun belonging to January out of Booy's hut. He also took a gun belonging to Klaas out of Jacob's hut, that is all he took.

her

(Signed.) ZITI ×

mark.

Witnesses :

    (Signed) W. A. HUDSON,
            J. G. VERITY.

Before me :

(Signed) B. H. HOLLAND,

Resident Magistrate.

    January, sworn, states :—I live at Blinkwater, on Tini Macomo's farm. I pay rent for being on his farm. I paid one cow, this was for one year. I was in Graham's Town when the remains of stolen cattle were found near our huts. I heard about it on my return, and missed a gun belonging to me. The last witness told me that Tini Macomo had taken it. I went to see Tini about it. He said he had taken it as the property of thieves. I saw it in his hut. I have not got my gun back yet.

his
(Signed)   JANUARY   ×
mark.

Witnesses .

(Signed)   W. A. HUDSON,
J. G. VERITY.

Before me :

B. H. HOLLAND,
Resident Magistrate.

Klaas, sworn, states :—I reside on Tini's farm at the Blinkwater. I was in Graham's Town when the remains of stolen cattle were found near our huts. I was told about it when I returned. I was also informed by Ziti that Tini had taken my gun. I found my gun missing. I went to Tini and asked him for the gun. I saw it in his hut. He said he would not give it to me ; that he had taken it with the cattle belonging to thieves. I have not yet recovered my gun.

his
(Signed)   KLAAS   ×
mark.

Witnesses :

(Signed)   W. A. HUDSON,
J. G. VERITY.

Before me :

(Signed)   B. H. HOLLAND,
Resident Magistrate.

Nomona, sworn, states :—I live at the Blinkwater on Tini's farm, at the same place as the previous witnesses. Less than a month ago I remember Tini coming to our huts. He took three guns out of the huts. One gun belongs to Gwanya, my father, one to Klaas, and one to January. He also took a number of cattle ; some belonged to Booy, now in gaol ; one belonged to "Gwanya." Tini said he took these things because we had given his place a bad name ; he meant by this that stolen property had been traced to our kraal.

his
(Signed)   NOMONA   ×
mark.

Witnesses :

(Signed)   W. A. HUDSON,
J. G. VERITY.

Before me :

(Signed)   B. H. HOLLAND,
Resident Magistrate.

Inspector's Office,
Fort Beaufort, 3rd February, 1878.

The Civil Commissioner, Fort Beaufort.

Sir,—Yesterday I proceeded to Blinkwater for the purpose of placing some men of the district police force at Mr. Snodgrass' farm. At the Blinkwater hotel a large number of natives were congregated, and amongst them Tini Macomo, who came up to me in a very insulting manner; said, "Eh, Booth, what you wants." I took no notice of him, and he left at once. In a short time I moved on, and overtook him and eight or nine of his people seated by the side of the road. He said something and beckoned to me. I turned towards him, and called one of the policemen to interpret. I said I had not come to see him, and could not talk with him, as he had not obeyed the message I brought him from the magistrate (to restore the cattle to the people he had taken them from). He replied he did not want to talk about cattle; he had not given them up; *he was Government;* he would let me see soon, and I must turn back.

I told him he must not talk in that way or he would have to be sent to Fort Beaufort. He said something about who would take him, and again told me to turn back and not go on to his ground that he had bought of Shaw; and after jumping round two or three times, flourishing his kerrie, he started off at a run through the drift towards his huts, followed by his people. I went through the drift and quietly on along the road, which passes about 150 yards beyond his huts. He was then standing in front of the hut, and about a dozen people seated in front of him. After passing Tini's huts I saw Siqoi Kazi (one of the men who was with Tini at the drift) at his hut, which is about 1,000 yards beyond Tini's. A woman or girl came out of the hut with a gun, which they gave to him, and he returned with it towards Tini's. On my return, some half-an-hour afterwards, I saw the same man leaving Tini's huts with the gun, and going in the direction of his own huts. Tini and the people were still in front of his hut on my return.

Tini had been drinking but was not drunk. He knew well what he was saying and doing. With regard to the report that Edmund Sandilli had been on a visit to Tini, I cannot hear of anything to confirm it; those I have spoken with deny his having been there.

I have, &c.,

(Signed)   B. BOOTH,
Inspector of Native Locations.

Benjamin Booth, being duly sworn, states :—That the contents of the foregoing letter are true and correct, and that the expressions made use of by Tini Macomo were interpreted by Cornelius Carlo.

(Signed)   B. BOOTH.

Sworn before me, this 20th day of February, 1878.

(Signed)   B. HOLLAND,
Resident Magistrate.

Cornelius Carlo, being duly sworn, states :—I understand the Kafir language, and heard Tini Macomo make use of the expressions mentioned in Mr. Booth's letter.

his

(Signed)   CORNELIUS × CARLO.

mark.

Sworn before me, this 20th day of February, 1878.

(Signed)   B. H. HOLLAND,

Resident Magistrate.

———— — —

At Fort Beaufort, on this 3rd day of February, 1878, before me, Ben Herbert Holland, Resident Magistrate for the District of Fort Beaufort,

Appeared James, who, being duly sworn, states :—I am a member of Mr. Blakeway's police. Yesterday I and seven others belonging to this force were stationed by Sub-Inspector Booth on the farm of one Snodgrass, which adjoins Tini Macomo's farm. After dark Tini Macomo came to the house with about one hundred men ; they were armed with guns and assegais. Tini said it was now war time ; he did not recognize Government. He said he would not allow policeman to remain there. He said if they apprehended any of his people war would be proclaimed. He said if he found a policeman anywhere near his farm he would stab him with an assegai. Tini's people pushed us about and divided us, and then we ran away. After we left two shots were fired. I left the station after breakfast this morning ; one of the policemen was missing then.

his

(Signed)   JAMES ×

mark.

Witnesses :

    J. S. VERITY.
    C. J. BLAKEWAY.

Before me,

(Signed)   B. H. HOLLAND,

Resident Magistrate.

————

Kandilli, being duly sworn, states :—I am a policeman in Mr. Blakeway's force. Yesterday seven of us were stationed by Sub-Inspector Booth on the farm of James Snodgrass. Last night Tini Macomo came to the station with about one hundred men armed with guns and assegais. Tini put his assegai up to our faces, and said do you know that I could stab you ; what are you doing here ? He said you have no ground here. We were not on his ground. He said he did not recognise Government. He said he had been long living in the mountains ; that the white people would not let him rest ; they had been hunting for him, and he was tired of the bush. He said no policeman was to cross the boundary on to his place ; he would not allow it, nor would he allow us to stay there. He said if any policemen came to his place he would do them harm. Tini and his people said they would kill us, so we ran away. When they left I heard two shots fired. One of the policemen named Zinzani is still missing.

his
(Signed)   KANDILI ×
mark.

Witnesses :

(Signed)   J. G. VERITY.
               C. F. BLAKEWAY.

Before me,
B. H. HOLLAND,
Resident Magistrate.

Copy.]

TELEGRAM FROM W. B. CHALMERS, ESQ., FORT BEAUFORT, TO THE HONOURABLE THE COLONIAL SECRETARY, KING WILLIAM'S TOWN.

23rd February, 1878.

The Blinkwater, Schelmkloof, and Waterkloof is a very intricate country, and our plan is to surround it and to clear it. This cannot be done unless we have a sufficient force, and thus at once quell the rebellion and prevent it spreading. In a country like that it would be folly to underestimate the power of the rebels to do mischief. Colonel Palmer wishes for at least 100 more European regular soldiers, so as not to leave Beaufort unprotected ; and provide sufficient convoy for wagons containing supplies to follow the force to the top of Schelmkloof, &c. ; as it is his intention that the movement should take place in the dead of night in lightest marching order, so that the whole should be in position at daylight. All have a hard day's work before them, and were the men weighted it could not be done. Everything is being carried on as quietly as possible, so as not to excite alarm, and to hurry matters would only risk failure.

The second column will only reach Fort Beaufort from King William's Town to-day, and the commissariat have nothing like sufficient supplies here as yet to enable the force to move out and commence operations. Besides, the burgher force to be employed are scattered, and require sufficient time to be in readiness. The radius of the circle necessary to be operated upon is at least eight miles, any portion of which unprotected might result in failure of our plans. I may mention that Colonel Palmer and I fully concur in our views, and we are both of opinion that the Fingo levies are neither so sufficient not so well armed as would be desirable. From the very commencement Colonel Palmer and I have had Mr. Holland in our consultations, and he agrees with our views. And we have also invited Blakeway and Booth, two very good men, to all our consultations.

To serve a warrant now on Tini Macomo or his brother is simply to be sacrificing the lives of such men as may be entrusted with the execution of such warrants. Our plans are to surround him, and if he and his people do not make a complete submission, then to attack. And whether they submit or not, our intention is to clear those fastnesses of Kafirs, and disarm them all. Let the Government now distinctly inform us whether or not they approve of this.

E 2

COPY OF ULTIMATUM.

Camp, Fort Fordyce,
14th March, 1878.

To Wittbooy Matshana.

1. The Government does not wish to shoot the Kafirs down if they submit to the orders of the Government.

2. On account of the great trouble which the Kafirs in Schelmkloof and Waterkloof have given for a long time past, the Government is determined that Kafirs shall no longer remain in these parts.

3. The Kafirs in the Blinkwater and Schelmkloof refused to clear out, the consequences to them have therefore been most disastrous.

4. If the Kafirs at the back of Fort Fordyce, and those in the Waterkloof, will submit and come to me, and give up their guns and asssgais, and leave this country quietly, they will not be interfered with, and I will give them passes to remove from there, cattle, women, and children, either to Kama's, Toi's, or Siwani's locations.

5. I give them till 12 o'clock noon to-morrow, to comply with this demand of the Government.

Send your answer by the bearer, "Philip," before 12 o'clock noon to-morrow.

(Signed)   W. B. CHALMERS,
Special Civil Commissioner.

A true copy:

(Signed)   H. W. PALMER,
Lieutenant-Colonel 90th Light Infantry.

———

Civil Commissioner's Office,
Fort Beaufort, 27th March, 1878.

The Honourable the Colonial Secretary, Cape Town.

SIR,—With reference to the recent operations at Tini Macomo's location Schemkloof, and the Waterkloof, I beg to enclose for your information copies of all telegrams and depositions, &c., in any way bearing upon the matter, up to the date of the arrival of Mr. Chalmers as special commissioner. These documents will speak for themselves, and will show what a lawless lot of people had been allowed to congregate at Tini Macomo's place, and on Mr. Shaw's farm, Schelmkloof. The farmers in this district had been brought to a state verging on desperation, through the repeated thefts of stock by the residents of these places; the nature of the country and the facilities afforded for concealing stock, making it almost impossible to bring the thefts home to the thieves. According to the documents I enclose you will see that on several occasions farmers and others, in search of stolen stock, were met with armed resistance, both on Tini's and Shaw's farms; also, that Tini arrogated to himself the powers possessed by a chief in Kafirland of confiscating the property of people upon the pretence that thefts had been traced to their kraal, no matter whether they were innocent or not, and that when ordered by me, through the inspector of his location, to restore the stock and guns, he refused to do so, saying he was Government. Further that he accompanied by a number of armed men, seditiously went to the adjoining farm belonging to Snodgrass, where a number of police had been stationed in order to intercept thieves, and threatened the lives of these men, causing them to vacate their posts. These matters were all reported to Government at the time, and as this state of things could not be tolerated steps similar to those at present on foot were ordered to be taken by the late ministry.

Upon your assuming office proceedings were stayed for a time; subsequently Mr. Chalmers was appointed special commissioner to inquire into the whole affair, with power to act. After perusing the documents I laid before him he came to the conclusion that the only remedy was to clear out this den of thieves. A warrant was issued by me against Tini Macomo for sedition, and against his brother for theft, on sworn affidavits. After consultation with Colonel Palmer and myself, Mr. Chalmers decided upon a plan to try and effect the capture of Tini Macomo and his brother, and to compel the Kafirs to clear out of that part of the country. With this in view the troops and irregular forces, under Colonel Palmer, left this on the night of Monday the 4th instant, with the intention of trying to surprise Tini, and apprehend him. We reached the Blinkwater Hotel about two o'clock in the morning, rain coming down in torrents all the way. A halt was made at Blinkwater for about two hours. We then proceeded to Tini's place, Booth, in charge of a number of rural police and a portion of Pope's Fingo Levy, having left the main body before reaching the Blinkwater, in order to search the huts in the neighbourhood of Fuller's Hoek, where one of Tini's brothers resided. Orders had been sent previously to different bodies of burghers and volunteers, to station themselves at the head of the different kloofs, to cut off retreat in every direction, and Captain Stevens, of the 90th Regiment, with a mountain gun, had been sent off some days previously in order to be in position at or near Shaw's school-house at the appointed time. As far as these arrangements are concerned I think they were well-planned and well-carried out. When we arrived within a mile of Tini's location, the Beaufort Rangers, supported by some of the Fingo police, were sent forward to quietly surround Tini's huts, and try and apprehend him. We arrived soon after this had been done; just at daybreak we found several Kafirs had been apprehended, with assegais in their hands, trying to escape; Tini himself not being there, his huts were burnt and the column proceeded in the direction of Snodgrass' farm. Whilst on their way an armed Kafir appeared on the hill above; he was fired at by some one, and immediately returned the fire, his bullet striking within a few yards of us. Shortly after this I accompanied Colonel Palmer to the farm of Snodgrass, in order to ascertain whether there was any good camping ground. The water supply being insufficient the Colonel returned, and had the tents pitched in the vicinity of Macomo's Kraal. Mr. Chalmers, who subsequently arrived, and I, remained at Snodgrass' farm. Whilst there some one came in to say that armed Kafirs were approaching. We went out and saw a number of Kafirs on the hill opposite; about fifteen volunteers went to meet them; a good many shots were exchanged, and after two of the Kafirs had fallen they retired, saying they would come back that night. In the evening we returned to camp. One of Tini's councillors having been taken prisoner, Mr. Chalmers requested him to take a message to Tini, to the effect that if he or any of his people surrendered, their lives would be spared. He agreed to this and left the same evening. The next morning we proceeded to the kloofs opposite Snodgrass. Several shells were thrown in, and afterwards the police and native levies were sent in to scour the bush. Whilst there the messenger sent the previous evening came out and stated that he could not find Tini, but that he had delivered the message to his brother Ngacaka. Kafirs were seen making away from these kloofs over into Sweetnam's The forces afterwards moved off in that direction. In passing Sweetnam's house we found that it had been burnt the previous night. One of the Beaufort Rangers had a narrow escape near this, being fired at by a Kafir at the head of one of the kloofs. When we arrived at Sweetnam's kloof we were informed that the place was swarming with Kafirs, and that they had opened fire on the burghers stationed near Fordyce that morning ; that a smart engagement had ensued, and that seven Kafirs had been killed, and many wounded, including two of Tini's brothers, Ngaka and Solomon. One of the Kafirs shot was found wearing the uniform stolen from Thurtle (see examination), and in possession of his rifle. Colonel Palmer ordered volleys to be fired into the kloofs at different ranges. Whether any of the enemy were killed is not known, but it had the effect of bringing a good many cattle into view, which were captured by the native levies. It being now late it was thought advisable to return to camp, Pope's levy being left to prevent the Kafirs escaping. The next morning all the deserted huts were burnt. Blakeway, with his police, was sent to assist Pope's levy in clearing the bush at Sweetnam's, but found it empty, the Kafirs evidently having decamped during the night. The troops and other forces proceeded up Blinkwater Hill and encamped at Cross' farm.

The following three days were spent in clearing the Schelmkloof. A few natives were shot, and some cattle captured. On Monday, the 11th instant, I returned to Fort Beaufort to attend to circuit court business, and the column moved on to Fort Fordyce, the following posts being left occupied, viz :—Snodgrass', Sweetnam's, and Cross'.

As far as my observation went I am of opinion that from the first the Kafirs intended to make a stand, from the fact of their deserting their huts, driving their cattle into the deep kloofs, and hiding their women and children away in the bush. They never expected that such a crushing force would be brought against them, but, after finding their case was hopeless, they retreated during the night time to the Waterkloof ; not a man surrendered himself.

Whatever interested parties may say to the contrary I feel convinced that this movement has been a splendid thing for the country generally, and will be the saving of this district if the country is permanently occupied by a number of Europeans ; to say nothing of the good it has done in preventing the ingress of Kafirs from the neighbourhood of the Amatolas, for I think it is pretty certain that, had they been worked out there, they would most probably have made for this part of the country, the number of cattle found showing that they would have been amply provided for in the way of commissariat supplies. It has also a good moral effect on the Kafirs living at the Umdala and Appies Drie, about whose loyalty I was very doubtful. They have nearly all voluntarily surrendered their arms, and I believe the Stockenstrom Kafirs are doing likewise.

In an expedition of this nature no doubt a few cases of hardship must arise, but these can be inquired into hereafter, and dealt with upon their merits.

I hope you will excuse the length of this report.

I have, &c.,

(Signed)   B. H. HOLLAND,
Civil Commissioner.

From Chalmers, Fort Fordyce, to Colonial Secretary, King William's Town.

25th March, 1878.

Yesterday I went with a company of infantry, two guns, and native levies to Mundell's Krantz ; shelled the kloofs to the right of Waterkloof, and sent the levies into the kloofs. Winterberg burghers went into the kloof lower down. Captain Pope with Fingoes was sent into Schelmkloof, and Sub-Inspector Chalmers and Captain Bowker sent with burghers and native police into the upper part of Waterkloof, into Arris Hoek, and along the kloof ranges. In all these localities the Kafirs are all cleared out, not a fresh spoor to be seen; farmers returning to their farms. To-day we go to Iron Mountain; to-morrow, as stated in my last telegram, go round to Maasdorp, &c., thence to Beaufort.

Several Kafirs at the western enterance of Waterkloof, who have been living quietly, have voluntarily given up their arms, and have requested passes to go into the midland districts for service, so as to be away from the disturbances of their countrymen.

Post Retief Kafirs have voluntarily given up their arms. Tini Macomo has cleared out with a very few followers, and has gone eastward, stated to have gone to Sandilli. Women and children have all been sent out. Several men, who were not only Tini's principal men, but who were leading men in the Macomo tribe, have been killed in the engagements.

I should like you to see sketch of the country by Lieutenant Cameron, which is being sent by post by Colonel Palmer to the General to-day. You will see positions of our posts. I am very desirous to hear about Sandilli's movements. If he does not break into here, then all will go on all right, as we have now complete possession of these fastnesses. The Government should try and get them out of the hands of private proprietors as soon as possible, and parcel them out in some small lots to such emigrants as the Germans, and have this country thickly populated by such industrious people. A commission might be appointed to negotiate with these proprietors.

Copy.]

FROM SECRETARY, NATIVE AFFAIRS, KING WILLIAM'S TOWN, TO COLONEL PALMER AND MR. CHALMERS, FORT BEAUFORT.

27th March, 1878.

I have given no authority for anyone to go into Schelmkloof, and if Mr. Chalmers and Colonel Palmer deem it desirable for military purposes that no natives should at present go into the kloof they will use their own judgment in refusing to allow it.

FROM SECRETARY, NATIVE AFFAIRS, KING WILLIAM'S TOWN, TO RESIDENT MAGISTRATE, FORT BEAUFORT.

27th March, 1878.

Please make a formal inquiry into capture of cattle belonging to R. E. Hards, in your district, and damage to his servant's property, and seizure of their cattle, and report here without delay.

Confidential.]

FROM SECRETARY, NATIVE AFFAIRS, KING WILLIAM'S TOWN, TO W. B. CHALMERS, FORT BEAUFORT.

27th March, 1878.

MY DEAR CHALMERS,—You are aware that several representations have been addressed to the Government in regard to what their writers term the illegality of the proceedings conducted under your charge.

I am, of course, not disposed to accept or endorse the statements which have been made, but I cannot impress upon you too urgently the necessity for bearing in mind that when martial law does not exist the civil power is dominant, and its requirements must be observed.

Relying upon your experience and judgment the Government has no doubt that in the conduct of the operations in the Fort Beaufort district the requirements of law have not only been observed, but any departure from them completely avoided. And they feel confident that you will be able to give such explanation of the circumstances under which you have acted as will remove all ground for complaining.

TELEGRAM FROM CHALMERS, BALFOUR, FORT BEAUFORT, TO SECRETARY FOR NATIVE AFFAIRS, KING WILLIAM'S TOWN.

29th March.

After placing all the men in our several posts round Schelmkloof and Waterkloof, Colonel Palmer and I left Fort Fordyce with remainder of column on the 27th, and arrived here yesterday. At request of the farmers, on the 27th I branched off with twenty-five mounted men, and visited the country along Winterberg and Kaal Hoek, and joined the column that evening at Upper Blinkwater.

Kafir servants and tenants all willingly and voluntarily gave up their arms, and wished to be considered as loyal.

Farmers all rejoiced at success of our operations at Schelmkloof and Waterkloof. Have returned to their farms, and commenced ploughing, and all state that a most wonderful change for the better has taken place among their Kafir servants and tenants.

Left ten Fingoes (levies) at Hartley's, and ten at Kaal Hoek to patrol from Upper Blinkwater to this.

Everything in a most satisfactory state. The Kafirs have all voluntarily and willingly given up their arms to their magistrate, Mr. Borcherds, and requested him to register them as loyal.

At Buxton and other places I met them, and spoke to them kindly, pointing out to them the advantages of a loyal, industrious, and honest life, and the disastrous consequences of disloyalty. They all appreciate this. Have met Mr. Borcherds, the Reverends Reid and Thomson. All speak in the highest terms of our successes at Schelmkloof and Waterkloof, and the good resulting therefrom; and all men of experience say we did not take possession of these fastnesses a day to soon, as Sandilli's intention was to make for them.

Our tour throught this way has done a great deal of good, has pleased everyone, and has restored confidence to all. We start from here to-day for Fort Beaufort, which it is our intention to reach to-morrow. There are fifty of the 24th, and thirty of the same regiment stationed at Snodgrass' and Cross' farms, at Schelmkloof. These, I believe, are to be relieved by the 90th from Beaufort and Fort Wellington. There are sixty of the 90th and a division of Royal Artillery at Fort Fordyce, and fifty of the same regiment at Botha's farm in Waterkloof. The remainder of the regiment and of the Royal Artillery must garrison Fort Beaufort. It will never do to leave Fort Beaufort ungarrisoned, and I do not see how a single man from the 90th regiment can be spared from the district of Fort Beaufort.

CHALMERS, TOP OF BLINKWATER HILL, FORT BEAUFORT, TO COLONIAL SECRE-
TARY, KING WILLIAM'S TOWN.

9th March, 1878.

Yesterday we worked up the rugged country into Schelmkloof proper the main column ; with two guns on the eastern side, and the burghers
with two guns and a company of infantry on the west, working round to
the high ground over Schelmkloof. The kloofs were well shelled as we
went along, and were afterwards well scoured by the native levies. We
met with no opposition except the firing of a few shots. There are still
some rebels in the basin at the head of the Schelmkloof, which basin is a
very extensive, rugged, and densely wooded country. We intended to
work this piece of country to-day, but our transport has been a complete
break down in coming up the Blinkwater hill yesterday, and is altogether
retarding our movements. The rebels have nearly all fled to the Maasdorp
Forest in the Stockenstrom district. Our forces are not sufficient to follow
them up, and at the same time to clear and hold this country and the
Waterkloof. With a view to keeping what we have already cleared, we
intend placing fifty soldiers and fifteen native policemen opposite Tini
Macomo's late kraal ; thirty native levies at the bottom of Sweetnam's
kloof ; thirty soldiers and some native police here. Cross, farm and fifty
soldiers with some native at Fort Fordyce. This will form a complete
circle round the track of country known as Schelmkloof. I trust the Government will take the necessary steps to have these points permanently
occupied by a sufficient number of F.A.M. Police, or otherwise by the
military. More cattle were captured out of the kloofs yesterday, and a
great many women and children were found. They have been brought
out and directed to leave this part. We have enabled to hear where Tini
Macomo has fled to. He and his brother were in one engagement, and
his brother is reported to be badly wounded. His principal counsellor is
a prisoner. It is a great pity our transport is so very bad : it prevents
operations being carried on actively.

CHALMERS, CROSS' FARM, FORT BEAUFORT, TO COLONIAL SECRETARY, KING
WILLIAM'S TOWN.

10th March, 1878.

Yesterday scoured the kloofs in the basin at the head of Schelmkloof ;
found only two men who showed fight, and were shot. Captain Pope, of
the Fingoes, slightly wounded accidentally in the hand by one of his men.
Found a very large number of women and children ; brought them all out.
We intend going through this part again to-morrow, to make sure that it
is clear, and thence on to Fort Fordyce. Very alarming reports which
gave me much anxiety were sent to me from Stockenstrom two days ago
about the natives there, that they intended rising ; and it was a question
with me whether we should not go there first instead of to Waterkloof. I
am glad to say that last night I received express from Borcherds and Rev.
Reid informing us that the natives had quieted down : that they were
merely terror-stricken at our two first day's operations here, and that they
apprehended no danger : also, that the rebels, who had fled from Schelmkloof and gone to Maasdorp Forest, had again left that part and gone towards Waterkloof. The country occupied by Tini Macomo and his followers, including Schelmkloof, has been well scoured. I have placed posts
all round in good commanding positions to keep occupation, and I hope the
Government will take immediate steps to prevent its again falling into the
hands of the Kafirs.

[Enclosure No. 1.]

Copy.]

Fort Beaufort, March 11, 1878.

B. H. Holland, Esq., Civil Commissioner and Resident Magistrate,
Fort Beaufort.

Sir,—I have the honour to state that I have been credibly informed that Samuel Chete, native day school teacher on Mr. Shaw's Farm, has been taken prisoner in the late operations of the military and colonial forces, in the neighbourhood of Fort Fordyce.

I beg to state that the said Samuel Chete is a Government paid agent, under my control. Mr. Shaw applied to me, as the Wesleyan superintendent of the Fort Beaufort circuit, to obtain a teacher for said farm. I applied to Dr. Dale, Superintendent-General of Education, for a grant, which was made in the usual way: upon which I obtained Samuel Chete, one of Kama's best men, also a local preacher and class leader in the Wesleyan Church. This selection was approved by Dr. Dale, upon which I located him upon Mr. Shaw's farm, where he has carried on the school ever since, being about the space of one year and a half; during which time he has conducted himself to my entire satisfaction. It was, therefore, with great surprise and regret that I learned that a few days ago he was taken prisoner, and, so far as I have the means of knowing, is still detained as such. I am responsible to Dr. Dale for the teachers under my charge receiving Government pay. I must beg very earnestly that this case be investigated forthwith, so that if Samuel Chete is guilty he may be committed accordingly, but if not guilty he may be discharged at once. I am not able to see Samuel Chete personally, but it is possible that his cattle have also been seized. If so, I must further beg that his cattle be restored without delay, and compensation made if any loss has been sustained.

I have the honour to be,
&c., &c.

[Enclosure No. 2.]

Copy.]

Fort Beaufort, March, 11, 1878.

B. H. Holland, Esq., Civil Commissioner and Resident Magistrate,
Fort Beaufort.

Sir,—I have the honour to inform you that since my letter of this morning, the prisoner Samuel Chete has been brought into town and lodged in prison, by order of the magistrate. I have seen the prisoner, from whom I obtain the following particulars of his capture :—He was in the house or hut where he lived, being a short distance from the school-room on the way towards Fort Fordyce, *but not near the bush*. There were also some women in the house, but no other man. Captain Mundle, a Dutchman, and some others, came and found him there. They asked whether he was a Kafir or a Fingo? He said a Kafir. They said you are our prisoner. He answered, but I am the schoolmaster. They swore at him, and said he was their prisoner. They then asked if there was any gun in the house? He said no ; there was only an assegai. They then searched his box, and threw about his clothes, and a new velisse (sic) which cost 15s. they took away with them. After this they ordered him to drive cattle and took him to Fort Fordyce. I have had to do with this man in many ways for nearly two years, and have never had the slightest ground to doubt his veracity or loyalty.

I have been informed that the hut or house had been burned down. If so Chete's books and clothes have been destroyed, which could not be valued at less than £20. He has paid me some £5 or £6 for some of the best books in the English language within a few months.

Being an Englishman, and a truly loyal subject, I most certainly protest against this man being kept in a prison yard in the pouring rain (the rain is pouring while I write), without cover or shelter, and hope that means may be found to liberate him at once. If this case well authenticated was to find its way into the hands of the Aboriginal Protection Society, it would have a very damaging effect upon the whole proceeding of the present harassing war.

I have the honour to be

&c., &c.

[Enclosure No. 3.]

Fort Beaufort, 13th March, 1878.

B. H. Holland, Esq., Civil Commissioner and Resident Magistrate,
Fort Beaufort.

SIR,—I have the honour to inform you that I have obtained some further particulars relative to Chete, the teacher, and the family with which he was living, which I think it desirable to lay before the Government.

Chete is not married, but was living with a family of the name of Hans, who are members of the Wesleyan Church. They are all Kama's Kafirs, and come from a sub-station in the Armshow circuit, called Emdeyeni, where I knew them.

Hans has about 40 or 42 cattle (since proved 42, horses 2, besides other goods), and hired a place to graze them on Mr. Shaw's farm. When the drought became severe he arranged or hired the liberty of grazing these cattle on the adjoining farm of Mr. Hartley. The arrangement was for Hans to go with the cattle and herd them, whilst Chete and the family remained at home, and Chete was in the house with the family when he was made prisoner. Hans was on Mr. Hartley's farm minding the cattle when they were swept off by some of the colonial forces. Hans was taken prisoner, and is now in gaol, having lost all.

I am aware that I have received this information from Chete alone, and it may be said that it is not true; but happily it is capable of being proved or disproved. As to their being members of my church, my own church books will prove that; and as to their coming from Emelizeni, and bringing their certificates of church membership with them I have written proof of that.

I need not say that these are very painful cases, and that already a number of Kama's people are feeling very sore about them. I hope there may be no delay in rectifying them, so far as possible.

I have the honour to be,

&c., &c.

Copy.]

[Enclosure No. 4.]

Civil Commissioner's Office,
Fort Beaufort, 13th March, 1878.

Rev. W. C. Holden, Fort Beaufort,

SIR,—With reference to your letter of this day's date, regarding the circumstances under which a man named Samuel Chete way apprehended, and forwarded to the gaol at this place, I beg to inform you that I have forwarded your letters to Mr. Chalmers, the special commissioner appointed by Government, and requested him to let me know whether there are any sufficient grounds for detaining this man in gaol. Mr. Chalmers being near the spot where the apprehension took place, will be able to make full inquiries into the matter. And I feel sure that he will see that justice is done. Copies of your previous letters were also forwarded to Mr. Chalmers.

I have, &c.,

[Enclosure No. 5.]

On Thursday the 14th I received the following note from Mr Holland :—

14th March, 1878.

MY DEAR SIR,—I have released Chete upon condition that for the present he does not return to Shaw's place. To this I returned the following answer.

Fort Beaufort, 14th March, 1878.

B. H. Holland, Esq., Civil Commissioner and Resident Magistrate,
Fort Beaufort.

SIR,—I have the honour to acknowledge the favour of your note of this morning, informing me of the release of Samuel Chete, the teacher, for which accept my thanks. His cattle were not at the place, but I would ask for £10 or £12 (see postscript) compensation towards his loss in clothes, books, &c. His crop of maize he will also lose, which would be of great value to him now that food is so dear.

I must beg you to do me the favour to forward to Mr. Chalmers my letter of yesterday, relating to the case of Hans. This man is no personal friend of mine, but as he and his family are members of my church we stand to each other in the relative positions of pastor and people, and I should be guilty of a serious dereliction of duty if I saw the labour of his life work swept away, and his family reduced to poverty, without making an effort through the proper channel to prevent such a catastrophe.

I am perfectly satisfied that he had no connection with Tini or his people whatever ; he was living on a private farm, the use of which he was paying for ; he was attending to his own business at a good distance from the scene of conflict, had not been warned of danger, and had consequently taken no steps to escape from it. If these facts are not so, Mr. Hartley can testify to their incorrectness, as the family of Hans is staying there whilst he is in prison. If he should return to Kama's tribe, stripped of everything, there will be a wound which will never heal, which at some time may break out in a very unfortunate way. I hope that he may not have to wait long before his liberation from prison is effected. Will you do me the favour to send this letter also to Mr. Chalmers.

I have the honour, &c., &c.

P.S. Chete asks if he can go to see what amount of goods are still left, as, since speaking to me, he has been informed that a new saddle and bridle have been taken which cost £6 10s. apart from all other things. I do not feel at liberty to say that he can go unless authorized by the magistrate.

[[Enclosure No. 6.]

On the 18th I received the following letter from the Resident Magistrate :—

Copy.]

Resident Magistrate's Office,
Fort Beaufort, 16th March, 1878.

Rev. W. C. Holden, Fort Beaufort.

Sir,—I have the honour to inform you that I have released Hans and his three sons, as after inquiry I feel satisfied that there were no sufficient grounds for their apprehension. It appears to be one of those unfortunate cases which will occur in an expedition of this kind, and which those on authority cannot prevent.

I have given Hans a pass to Mr. Chalmers, who will, I feel sure, do all in his power to assist him in recovering his stock, &c. ; none of the cattle captured in that part of the country were sent to Fort Beaufort.

I have, &c.

[Enclosure No. 7.]

Fort Beaufort, 17th March, 1878.

B. H. Holland, Esq., Civil Commissioner and
Resident Magistrate, Fort Beaufort.

Sir,—I have the honour to acknowledge your letter of the 16th inst., informing me of the release of Hans and his three sons from prison, as also giving Hans a pass to Mr. Chalmers to assist him in recovering his stock, for which accept my thanks. I now enclose an application to Mr. Chalmers for compensation to Chete and Hans for their losses, if you will kindly forward the same.

[Enclosure No. 8.]

I then wrote the following to Mr. Chalmers :—

Fort Beaufort, March 19, 1878.

W. B. Chalmers, Esq., Special Commissioner, &c., &c.

Sir,—I have the honour to inform you that through Mr. Holland, the resident magistrate, I have obtained the release of Samuel Chete, teacher, and Hans and his three sons from prison. I now beg to request that at as early a period as possible full compensation may be made for the losses they have sustained. Hans had 42 cattle, one grey mare, and one young stallion, swept away, besides the ruining of his two horses, together with various other effects connected therewith.

Chete had no cattle, there but has lost considerably in his personal effects. He desires permission to go out and see what has been destroyed or taken away, so that he may be able to make a definite statement of his losses.

I have the honour, &c.

[Enclosure No. 9.]

Camp, Fort Fordyce,
20th March, 1878.

FROM LIEUTENANT COLONEL H. W. PALMER, 90th FOOT, COMMANDING THE
TROOPS, FORT BEAUFORT DISTRICT, AND THE SPECIAL COMMISSIONER TO
THE REV. CLIFFORD HOLDEN, WESLEYAN MINISTER, FORT BEAUFORT.

SIR,—In reply to your letter of the 19th instant, we have the honour
to inform you (as Mr. Holland at our request has no doubt already done)
that we have not the remotest intention of countenancing the slightest
injustice towards any one by the imperial and colonial forces under our
direction ; and, while regretting any injustice or hardship towards Hans
and Samuel Chete, we beg to inform you that the acts of which these men
complain were committed by a Mr. Mundle, of Tarkastadt, on his own
responsibility, and that he was not acting under our orders or instructions,
nor did he at the time belong to our forces.

At the same time every assistance has been afforded by us to Hans,
and others who have suffered from Mr. Mundle's acts, to recover their
property.

Mr. Booth informs us that of the 42 head of cattle claimed, 12 were
reported to him at the last registry as sold, or otherwise dispose of.

We have, &c.,

(Signed)　　H. W. PALMER, Lieutenant-Colonel, 90th Foot,
　　　　　　　　Commanding the Troops, Fort Beaufort District.

(Signed)　　W. B. CHALMERS,
　　　　　　　　Special Commissioner.

————

Copy.]　　　　　　　　[Enclosure No. 10.]

Fort Beaufort, March 26th, 1878.

Lieut.-Colonel H. W. Palmer, and W. B. Chalmers,
　　Special-Commissioner, &c., &c., &c.

Camp, Fort Fordyce.

SIR,—I have the honour to acknowledge the receipt of your letter of
the 20th instant upon the case of Samuel Chete and Hans. I was not
aware before that Mr. Mundle was acting " without orders or instructions "
from the authorities commanding the expedition in the Waterkloof.

I am fully conscious that the authorities did not intend or design to
inflict unnecessary suffering and damage upon these parties, but the
painful facts are these notwithstanding, and this renders the claim to
immediate reparation the stronger. Although the action of Mr. Mundle
was not authorized I hold that it was *indorsed* by those conducting these
operations. The cattle, I presume, were taken to Fort Fordyce among
others, but if not, *the men were taken there and detained prisoners with the
rest.* They were afterwards sent into Fort Beaufort in company with others,
and lodged in gaol, and when I applied to the magistrate to allow me to get
Chete out on bail, he refused, as this was a case of rebellion, and he did
not feel at liberty to act until Mr. Chalmers, the commissioner, came in. I
therefore submit that the authorities, and not Mr. Mundle, are responsible.

The view that I take of the matter is,—that it was illegal to take men prisoner's and confiscate their property upon private farms in the absence of any breach of the peace on the parts of the proprietors of said farms. Also, that it was illegal in reference to the men themselves, who, whilst keeping the laws of the colony, were entitled to the protection of said laws.

But if accidently or undesignedly their persons have been incarcerated in prison, and their property destroyed, there should be no delay in the restoration of such property and the reparation of such damage.

What I now write relates distinctly to the persons named in this correspondence; and not to Tini, or his farm, or his people, or his acts; but to European farmers and those Kafirs who dwelt by right upon their farms. Neither must it be understood that I do this out of any connection with Mr. Shaw. That gentleman bought his farms and disposed of them as he thought best without any reference to me. I do not meddle with politics or other peoples affairs in this correspondence, but deal simply with the case of my own church members, who have a right to look to me for such assistance as it may be in my power to give. Probably £20 would cover the greater claims of Chete, and Hans could have his losses made up out of cattle taken, which would be otherwise sold. I should feel it a great relief if this painful case could be satisfactorily settled as soon as possible.

I have, &c.,

(Signed)   W. CLIFFORD HOLDEN.

[Enclosure No. 77.]

Copy.]

Fort Beaufort, 2nd April, 1878.

FROM LIEUTENANT-COLONEL H. W. PALMER, 90TH FOOT, COMMANDING THE TROOPS, FORT BEAUFORT DISTRICT, TO THE REVEREND CLIFFORD HOLDEN, FORT BEAUFORT.

SIR,—I beg to acknowledge receipt of your letter of the 26th ultimo, and to inform you that Han's cattle and those of his brother and sons have been restored to him, according to the number which they had registered, and any claims to cattle not registered I regret to say cannot be entertained.

If Chete will send in a list of his articles, which were destroyed, or seized, and a valuation of the same, his claim will be taken into consideration.

I have, &c.,

(Signed)   H. D. PALMER,
Lieutenant Colonel 90th Foot,
Commanding the Troops Fort Beaufort District.

40

[Enclosure No. 12.]

Copy.]

CLAIMS OF CHETE, DAY SCHOOL TEACHER, FOR PROPERTY DESTROYED BY VOLUNTEERS.

	£	s.	d.
1. New saddle and bridle	6	10	0
1. Vallise	0	15	0
New English books, including commentary on the Bible, 20s., and Biblical Muséum 27s. 6d, with others, all destroyed	6	0	0
Mr. Mildenhall told me that he saw all these books in the School-house the morning after Chete was taken prisoner, that one book looked as if worth 20s., which was exactly the amount paid for it; the amounts of the others are taken from my books.			
Loss of clothes and other goods, as he was taken away with only the clothes he stood up in and had no opportunity of getting his things	6	15	0
Three large acres of mealies destroyed, at low computation, say 6 bags, at 40s. per bag	12	0	0
People's parts of salary for 12 months which they cannot now pay as their property is destroyed and the school broken up	10	0	0
	£42	0	0

HANS.

42 cattle and 18 calves, including young things, total 60, of these 36 have been returned. Still claimed, 22 cattle and 2 calves. Two houses with wagon gear in them belonging to Hans, and one house belonging to his sisters were all burned down.

KLAAS.

10 cattle and 7 calves were taken, total 17. Returned, 7 cattle and 2 calves. Still claimed, 3 cattle and 5 calves; 1 house and property all burned down.

The above particulars I have taken personally from the parties named. They are not at hand for me to obtain their own signatures, but if required, these I will obtain if their modified claims are complied with as stated in my letter.

(Signed)   W. CLIFFORD HOLDEN,
Wesleyan Minister.

[Enclosure No. 13.]

FROM REV. W. C. HOLDEN TO LIEUTENANT-COLONEL PALMER, 90TH F., COMMANDING THE TROOPS, FORT BEAUFORT DISTRICT.

Fort Beaufort, April 4th, 1878.

SIR,—I have the honour to acknowledge your letter of the 2nd instant, relating to Chete, Hans, and his brother Klaas; these men were in my study when your letter arrived, and I spoke to them upon its contents. In enclosure No.—I give a statement of Chete's losses, which amounts to £42. I have requested him by way of compromise to accept £30, which he has consented to do.

The claims of Hans in said enclosure are also given. He says that he gave in these claims to Mr. Booth, who refused to register them, only admitting 36, which is the number he has received in return, as also his two horses.

Klaas makes the same statement as his brother Hans, that he gave in his number, 17, including calves, but Mr. Booth refused to register more than ten. They further say that when sent to Baviaan's River in search of stock, they saw them all with the exception of one cow and one young ox. They both consent to forego their claims for the restoration of their houses and goods, but require the whole of their cattle.

When His Excellency the Governor was in Fort Beaufort, I explained to him fully the cases of Chete and Hans. He asked if I had brought them to the notice of Mr. Ayliff. I answered no ; as I was anxious to have these settled by the local authorities if I could. He then advised me to make Mr. Ayliff acquainted with them, which I said I would do as I had all the documents in perfect order. Just before your letter arrived I had completed the regular official preparation of the documents of the case, with copies of all the enclosures (ten in number) and was about to post them. But upon the receipt of your letter I conversed at length with the parties concerned, with the results stated in this letter. I will now delay the forwarding of the documents to Mr. Ayliff a few days, to see if the claims above stated are complied with, if not, I will then forward the documents to Mr. Ayliff that they may be ready to be placed before Parliament. I shall regret if I am obliged to do this, as I am persuaded our new ministry will have enough to do to get through the business of Parliament, and I think this clear case with its moderate claims would have a very prejudicial effect upon all the parties concerned.

I have, &c.

Copy.] [Enclosure No. 14]

Fort Beaufort, April 2nd, 1878.

The Honourable William Ayliff, Secretary of Native Affairs,
      Cape Colony.

SIR,—I have the honour to forward copies of enclosures on the cases of Chete, a teacher, and Hans and his family, who were taken prisoners from the farms of Messrs. Shaw and Hartly, in connection with the recent hostile operations in the Waterkloof. The enclosures will fully explain the circumstances and facts of these cases, upon which I beg further to add that, on the recent visit of His Excellency the Governor, he gave me a courteous and full hearing of these cases, and advised me to bring the subject before your notice, which I now do.

His Excellency, in conversation, pointed out the great hardship and loss of a number of farmers in British Kaffraria, missionaries and others. But I submit with all deference that these cases were not paralled. There open war and declared rebellion prevailed, and the parties were duly notified thereof, so that they might make their escape. Here there was no war nor declared rebellion, so far as these men were concerned, *nor did these men live at the scene of operations, nor were they in any way mixed up with them*, and yet in a moment, *without warning*, a company of armed Europeans came upon them whilst peacefully pursuing their daily avocations : destroyed their property, drove away their cattle, and took them prisoners ; putting them in the prison yard without covering, where they must have still remained as common rebels until this day, had it not been for my untiring efforts in getting them out of prison.

Then again Chete, the teacher, was a special case even in this exceptional one, as he was not there for his own personal advantage in grazing cattle, &c., but was employed as my servant under Government for the benefit of the people.

I have been long in the country and have known something of three dreadful Kafir wars, but I have not known anything like this. In other wars the Kafirs have burnt down the houses and destroyed the property of the colonists ; but colonists did not seize loyal Kafirs, destroy their property and put them in prison. If then this conduct is not approved by the Government of the country, this should be at once proved by the most ample restoration of their property. It has been tacitly admitted by their release from prison, but compensation for the wrong and injustice inflicted has not yet been made.

It may be said that the farmers were also great sufferers ; yes, but their property was not seized and their persons sent to gaol as *rebels*. These might be called the accidental appendages or consequences of the expedition, *not* a deliberate, open seizure of their persons and property by force.

I enclose an approximate account of their losses in the hope that speedy reparation may be made.

I have, &c.,

W. CLIFFORD HOLDEN.

CHALMERS, FORT FORDYCE, TO COLONIAL SECRETARY, KING WILLIAM'S TOWN.

13th March, 1878.

Heavy fog and rain still continue ; unable to make any move ; I intend sending messenger to the Kafirs mentioned in my last telegram, telling them that if they, and those in Waterkloof, give up their arms and move quietly out of this country, they will not be interfered with, and that they can go to Kama's, Toise's, or Siwani's locations with proper passes. If they do not take advantage of this, we must only use force. Our success in the Blinkwater and Schelmkloof has had a most beneficial effect all round. The farmers are delighted at it, and they are all of opinion that the Waterkloof Kafirs will take advantage of the offer to be made to them. If they accept it, it will prevent hostilities spreading, and will show them that our object is not to slaughter them but to insist upon their complying with the demands of the Government, the object of which is their own good and the peace of the country. The farmers and their servants who are friendly and industrious Kafirs say that they already feel a security now that Schelmkloof, etc., has been cleared, which they have not experienced for many a long day. So soon as the weather permits, we intend making one more scouring of Sweetnam's and adjoining kloofs, to make sure that all is clear there.

CHALMERS, FORT FORDYCE, FORT BEAUFORT, TO COLONIAL SECRETARY, KING WILLIAM'S TOWN.

16th [March ?] 1878.

To-day have again thoroughly scoured Sweetnam's and the adjoining kloofs ; all clear. Patrols have also been out from the different posts. No Kafirs found. I hope the subject is being considered as to how Schelmkloof and the country about is to be occupied in future, so as to prevent its again falling into the possession of Kafirs. Raining very hard Friday night.

CHALMERS, FORT FORDYCE, TO COLONIAL SECRETARY, KING WILLIAM'S TOWN.

[17th March?] 1878.

I gave the Kafirs at the entrance of Waterkloof, Iron Mountain, and Waterkloof, every chance to surrender and give up their arms. I gave them three days up to 12 o'clock on Friday, but they failed to comply. We then made preparations to surround them and make a combined attack upon them. On Friday night in heavy rain we sent off burgher forces, volunteers, and company of infantry, to take up position at western side of Iron Mountain, and to be in position round west and north-west at 4 o'clock yesterday morning. At 3 o'clock yesterday morning 2 guns and infantry were sent to take up position along the eastern ridges. At the same hour the main column went down with two guns, the twelfth pass to take up position along the south and south-west, placing volunteers to cut off retreat from Waterkloof into either Arrie's Hoek or Schelmkloof. Notwithstanding the heavy ground, all were in position at the appointed hour. The Kafirs opened fire on the burghers on the southern side, but they were very soon demolished. The cannon on both sides did good service. The war cry was raised, but no response was given. The Kafirs were panic-struck, and took to the kloofs, leaving their cattle. We captured about 400 head of cattle, about 20 horses, and about 100 sheep and goats. The kloofs were well shelled by the artillery, and the European infantry searched them with volleys of musketry. The levies and burghers were then sent in and scoured the kloofs well. Several Kafirs shot. No casualty on our side. We so overpowered them and smashed them up that they did not attempt to rally at the Iron Mountain, which is the Waterkloof stronghold. We intend to keep occupation by stationing a company of soldiers and native police at Botha's farm, north of Iron Mountain, and a strong body of police at Moss's farm to the east of the mountain. We also contemplate establishing a post S.W. of the mountain. Schelmkloof, Sweetnam's Kloof, &c., are all clear, and having struck this blow at the Waterkloof we do not see that there is anything else to be done but for the Government to establish a good mounted European police force to patrol the country and catch thieves. Our determination and success at Schelmkloof and Waterkloof has struck terror among the natives in these parts. To show this, I need only mention the fact of the Kafirs at Umdala and Appies Draai near Fort Beaufort voluntarily giving up their arms to Holland, and requesting to be registered as loyal. The same chance ought to be offered them through their magistrates in other districts. I am thinking of going to the Kafirs at Macanzima and disarming them. On Friday evening the Waterkloof Kafirs attacked a farmer's place and carried off his cattle. We recaptured them all yesterday. All worked well yesterday. I cannot speak too highly of the good service done by the artillery. After our operations were finished, we had a dreadful march back to this over the mountains on account of very heavy thunderstorms. We intend sending a strong patrol over the same ground to-morrow.

———

CHALMERS, FORT BEAUFORT, TO COLONIAL SECRETARY, KING WILLIAM'S TOWN.

20th March, 1878.

Returned last night. Was eleven hours in the saddle on Monday, and fifteen yesterday. Very satisfactory trip, and am glad I went myself. Mr. Ayliff will know the country I went over. Went down Waterkloof, over Bush Neck, thence to the Kroonap, down the Kroonap, thence across to Macanzima to Field-cornet Leppans up Doornkloof to Olifant's Bush,

2

crossed the mountains back to Macanzima (?), up the Macanzima to Bennet's, thence to bottom of Winterberg round by Kaal Hoek, and so on back to this. The Waterkloof is all clear and only wants patrolling. Farmers all highly pleased at our operations here, and they all feel the beneficial effects of these operations already. On all the farms the Kafirs are now perfectly quiet. Such of them, as I thought it necessary to disarm, gave up their guns most willingly and expressed their wish to live peaceably. They have been taught such a lesson, and things have so changed for the better, that at one farm I found Kafirs in charge of valuable ostriches belonging to their masters. Field-cornet Leppan, a very intelligent and experienced man, was of great assistance to me. He, as well as the other farmers, told me that the good results of our success at Schelmkloof and Waterkloof are almost incredible, that all their servants have settled down quietly, and are now quite different men : that before our operations they were all unsettled, and that the evident intention was that Sandilli was to come and take possession of the Schelmkloof and Waterkloof, and that all these people were to make a raid upon the farmers, and join him with a large commissariat in these strongholds : that we did not commence our operations nor take possession of these fastnesses a day too soon, but that our determined operations have caused the Kafirs to settle down quietly. People could not be more thankful than the farmers all round. We are fortunate in taking possession of these fastnesses without any casualty on our side, and we must now keep possession once and for all. Thanks for your telegram of the 18th. Under the greatest hardships and difficulties all have worked cheerfully and willingly, and the most pleasant harmony has existed between the officers and men of Her Majesty's troops and those of the colony. We are having the country well patrolled to prevent Sandilli coming into the fastnesses we have won ; we have captured altogether about 2,000 head of cattle, 50 horses, and 400 sheep.

CHALMERS, FORT FORDYCE, TO COLONIAL SECRETARY, KING WILLIAM'S TOWN.

22nd [March ?], 1878.

We have a strong party out with 2 guns, patrolling country east of Schelmkloof, so as to be prepared for any movement of Sandilli's this way. Yesterday we went out with a large party and one gun down the 12th pass, and round the Waterkloof to the west of Iron Mountain, thence along the Kroom Range. All clear. We have stationed all our posts except one at the western entrance of Waterkloof. We are now in complete profession of Schelmkloof and Waterkloof. All that is now required is constant patrolling to stop any thieving which is sure to be carried on ; and I shall be glad when we are furnished with a force of F.A.M. Police. Magistrate of Stockenstrom reports that the Kafirs in his division are thoroughly cowed, owing to our success in Schelmkloof and Waterkloof. The practice of farmers allowing Kafirs to squat as tenants on their farms must be knocked on the head in this part of the country. The Kafirs pay good rents, but they only steal to enable them to do so, and they lead an idle and mischievous life. There must be some strict legislation on this very important subject. Please let us know sharp about Sandilli's movements, and ask Civil Commissioner, Fort Beaufort, to send express to us. Everything going on very satisfactorily here. Raining very heavily and bitterly cold.

RESIDENT MAGISTRATE, FORT BEAUFORT, TO SECRETARY OF NATIVE AFFAIRS, KING WILLIAM'S TOWN.

4th April, 1878.

Have kept back all claimed cattle from sale. Shall go into the proofs on Saturday. Presume the Government does not wish me to restore cattle to those who were in any way mixed up with Tini or the Schelmkloof people. Should like definite instructions about this. Just informed that one of our men shot dead by enemy at Schelmkloof.

———

CHALMERS, FORT BEAUFORT, TO HON. COLONIAL SECRETARY, KING WILLIAM'S TOWN.

28th [March?], 1878.

We shall have 150 of Blakeway's Fingo police, 200 Fingo levies recently enrolled under Pope. In these are included the 70 Fingoes sent by the Civil Commissioner of Seymour. Then we shall have about 150 Hottentots from Balfour neighbourhood. We shall thus have about 500 native footmen. I think we can manage with these. Colonel Palmer concurs.

———

CHALMERS AND COLONEL PALMER, FORT FORDYCE, TO SECRETARY NATIVE AFFAIRS, KING WILLIAM'S TOWN.

27th March, 1878.

Shaw of Fort Beaufort says that you have written to him that the people on his farm will be compensated for all losses of pots, etc., etc. We shall most certainly protest against such compensation. We might as well think of compensating Sandilli's and Kreli's people for their losses. The Kafirs here acted as rebels: they refused to surrender, raised the war-cry, and first opened fire upon us, and they must only stand the consequences.

———

R. E. HARDS, FORT BEAUFORT, TO SECRETARY NATIVE AFFAIRS.

26th March, 1878.

I have to report for your information, that some of the forces under Colonel Palmer and Mr. Chalmers, proceeded to my farm yesterday, took my servants and their families prisoners, burnt their huts and took their cattle, and this morning forcible possession was taken of my own cattle, which were in my enclosure. Such illegal and unjustifiable proceedings cannot be overlooked. I shall hold the Government liable for the value of my own cattle as well as my servants, and also for damages. Have reported the matter to the magistrate here.

———

CHALMERS, FORT FORDYCE, TO COLONIAL SECRETARY, KING WILLIAM'S TOWN.

23rd [March?], 1878.

As already reported, we are now in complete possession of the Schelmkloof, Waterkloof, etc. We keep up constant patrolling, but all is clear, and everything going on satisfactorily. We have stationed posts all round to keep possession, and give strict written instructions to the officers in charge of the posts what to do. We will leave fifty men of the 90th with two guns and twenty native police here. Unless we receive unfavourable news regarding Sandilli, Colonel Palmer and I, with the remainder of the forces not stationed on the posts, and two guns, will leave this on Tuesday and make a patrol round to Buxton, Balfour, Seymour, Maasdorp Forest, etc., in the Stockenstorm district, thence to Fort Beaufort. This will take us about five days. I throw it to you as a hint that tickets of citizenship should be abolished. They have been the source of great mischief. I hope the prevention of Kafirs squatting on farms in this part of the country, and the future occupation of these fastnesses will not be lost sight of by the Government.

CHALMERS AND COLONEL PALMER, FORT BEAUFORT, TO SECRETARY NATIVE AFFAIRS, KING WILLIAM'S TOWN.

26th [March ?], 1878.

Mr. Shaw of Fort Beaufort gives it forth that he holds a letter from you stating that the Kafirs who have been turned out of Schelmkloof, etc., are to be allowed to return there and reap their crops when ripe. Surely the Government would not do such a foolish thing after the trouble and hardships we have had to clear these fastnesses and take possession of them. If so, we might as well remove all the posts we have established to keep possession. Such an idea is so contrary to the communications we have had from the Colonial Secretary that we can hardly credit this report.

CHALMERS, FORT FORDYCE, TO COLONIAL SECRETARY, KING WILLIAM'S TOWN.

Yesterday I went with a company of infantry, two guns, and native levies to Mundell's Krantz, shelled the kloofs to the right of Waterkloof and sent the levies into the kloofs. Winterburg burghers went into the Waterkloof lower down. Captain Pope with Fingoes was sent into Schelmkloof, and Sub-Inspector Chalmers and Captain Bowker were sent with burghers and native police into the upper part of Waterkloof, into Arries' Hoek, and along the Kroome range. In all these localities the Kafirs are all cleared out—not even a fresh spoor to be seen. Farmers returning to their farms. To-day we go to Iron Mountain, and to-morrow as stated in my last telegram we go round to Maasdorp, etc., thence to Beaufort. Seven Kafirs at the western entrance of Waterkloof, who have been living quietly, have voluntarily given up their arms, and have requested passes to go into the Midland districts for service, so as to be away from the disturbances of their countrymen. Post Retief Kafirs have voluntarily given up their arms. Tini Macomo has cleared out with a very few followers and has gone eastward ; stated to have gone to Sandilli. Women and children have all been sent out. Several men who were not only Tini's principal men, but who were leading men in the Macomo tribe, have been killed in the engagements. I should like you to see sketch of the country by Lieutenant Cameron, which is being sent by post by Colonel Palmer to the General to-day. You will see the positions of our posts. I am very anxious to hear about Sandilli's movements. If he does not break into here, than all will go on all right, as we have now complete possession of these fastnesses. The Government should try and get them out of the hands of private proprietors as soon as possible, and parcel them out in small lots to such immigrants as the Germans, and have the country thickly populated by such industrious people. A commission might be appointed to negotiate with these proprietors.

Fort Beaufort, 2nd April, 1878.

The Honourable the Colonial Secretary, Cape Town.

SIR,—With reference to your letter, No. 272, of 13th February last, to my report to you dated—February; and to your letter of 20th of same month, and also to the several telegrams that passed between the Government and myself up to the 4th of March, I have now the honour to report that Colonel Palmer and myself, assisted by several gentlemen of experience and acquainted with this district, prepared our plans to carry out the instructions of the Government, in reference to Tini Macomo and his followers, and in clearing the country known as Schelmkloof and Waterkloof.

The accompanying annexure, marked A, will show the disposal of our forces and the respective positions to be taken up by them in commencing our operations. All were to be in position at 3 o'clock on the morning of the 5th March. At 9 o'clock on the night of the 4th March, Colonel Palmer and I with the main column left Fort Beaufort. The march was a most trying one to all, as it rained heavily the whole night. A little before daylight on the morning of the 5th instant, I sent Mr. Blakeway, together with the Beaufort Rangers, in advance with the warrants which had been issued for the apprehension of Tini Macomo and his brother Ngaka, with instructions to surround Tini's kraal, and to call upon him to surrender.

On the arrival of the party they found that Tini and his brother had fled, it having been stated that notice of our movements had been sent to them from Fort Beaufort, and that they and their principal men had gone into the dense kloof opposite Snodgrass's farm. The few men who remained surrendered themselves and gave up their arms. We kept these prisoners, and sent the women and children to Fort Beaufort.

We encamped at the Biinkwater. Some of our forces moved towards the kloof where Tini had taken up his position; the war-cry was raised by the Kafirs, and they fired upon the Balfour men who were at Snodgrass's farm, calling out to them, and defying them.

On account of the very inclement weather, however, instructions were issued to the forces not to make any movement.

Among the prisoners who surrendered at Tini's kraal was one of his principal counsellors, named Gwanishe. I therefore sent this man on the 5th March to Tini and his brother, calling upon them to surrender, strongly advising them to do so, and to call upon their followers to come out of the bush, and I would give them a safe passport out of those fastnesses for themselves, their families, and their stock. This man returned that night, stating that Tini was further up the kloof, and that he had not time to go so far, but that he had found his brother and his followers, and delivered my message to them; that his brother had sent on the message to Tini that night, and had requested Gwanishe to return next morning for the reply.

Next morning early I again sent off Gwanishe, who returned that afternoon, stating that they positively refused to surrender, and threatened to shoot him or any one else who should be sent to them again.

There was thus no help for it now, but to go on and take active measures against the hostile and rebellious attitude taken up by Tini and his followers.

Gwanishe reported to me that Tini and his followers were all armed and were determined to fight.

The rain continued incessantly up to the afternoon of the 6th, when the weather cleared. It was a most trying time for all, but every one bore the hardships cheerfully.

On the 7th, the main column moved to the kloof opposite Snodgrass's, but Tini and his followers had left it, raised the war-cry, and went with their cattle over into Sweetnam's Kloof, which is a very dense fastness.

The women and children whom we found in this kloof were sent off to Fort Beaufort. Some cattle were captured, and we destroyed the kraals which had been deserted by the rebels. We then followed them up to Sweetnam's kloof, they opened fire upon us, and several of them were shot.

They took up position with their cattle in the dense bush at the head of the kloof, and the guns under Captain Stevens shelled the kloof from the western side. The rebels, headed by Tini, left this position, and made for Aries' Hoek. On leaving this fastness they opened fire on Bowker's Rovers, when a very smart engagement took place, resulting in twelve rebels being killed and several wounded; among the latter, I was afterwards informed by the women, was Ngaka. About one thousand head of cattle were captured, and about forty Kafirs made prisoners.

Tini and the remainder of the people evidently made their way to Waterkloof. We searched Sweetnam's kloof well with shells and infantry musketry, and then sent in the native levies. On being satisfied that it was clear of rebels, we returned to our camp.

On the 8th we broke up our camp, and moved up the Blinkwater Hill. Our forces surrounded the lower part of Schelmkloof, searched it well with shell and musketry, and then sent the levies into the bush. We met with little opposition, the rebels making their way to the upper part of the Schelmkloof, which is a densely wooded and very rugged basin, and the hot-bed of all the thieving which has been so very extensively carried on here for many years. We captured some cattle, and found a great many women and children in the bush, and these we sent off to Fort Beaufort.

We encamped at Cross's farm, to the east of Schelmkloof, but in consequence of the wet state of the Blinkwater Hill our wagons could not reach us, and all had in consequence to put up with a great deal of inconvenience and hardship.

On the 9th we scoured the Schelmkloof basin, but from the spoors the rebels had evidently taken to Waterkloof. Two men were found who fired upon the Fingoes and were shot. A very large number of women and children were found, and were sent to Fort Beaufort.

On account of the heavy rain and dense fog we could do nothing on the 10th.

On the 11th we again sent in our forces into Schelmkloof and adjoining kloofs, but found them perfectly clear of Kafirs. We then established posts at Snodgrass's, at Sweetnam's, and Cross's farms, to keep possession of the Schelmkloof fastnesses which we had won. We then moved on to Fort Fordyce, where the remainder of the forces were to concentrate. We saw large numbers of cattle at the Waterkloof, and Kafirs congregated about the Iron Mountain in the Waterkloof. Being doubtful whether this was a sign of defiance or of peace, I thought it best to give them a chance to surrender. I thereupon, on the evening of the 12th, sent some Kafir women to these people, telling them to send three of their principal men over to me on the following morning, as I wished to speak to them. The women returned next morning, stating that the Kafirs declined sending over any one as they were afraid, and that I was to send some Europeans over to them to tell them what I had to say.

On the 13th I sent a young Kafir over to tell these people that if they

surrendered and gave up their arms, and moved quietly out of these fastnesses, they should not be interfered with, but that I would give them passes
to remove with their women and stock. This young man returned, stating
that they refused to surrender. He further informed me that Tini and his
brother were with these people.

Fearing that, in consequence of his youth, this messenger may not
have delivered my message correctly, on the 14th I sent two Kafirs who
had surrendered in Schelmkloof to deliver the same message, and also to
deliver to these people a similar written message in Kafir and in English
(copy enclosed, marked B), and signed by Colonel Palmer and myself.

These two men never returned, and I afterwards learnt from the
women found at the Iron Mountain, that the message and papers were not
only delivered to these people, but that the papers were read to Tini and
all the men by a Kafir who could read both English and Kafir ; that a few
of them were in favour of surrendering, but that Tini and the great majority
refused to do so, and threatened to kill the two men if they attempted to
return to us.

From the 11th to the 14th we had heavy rain and very dense fog, so
that it was impossible to do anything.

On the 14th the rebels were very defiant, coming out on the open
ground in the Waterkloof and having a war dance, and calling out, and
daring us to attack them.

I now learn from trustworthy native sources that the object of Tini and
the Waterkloof and Schelmkloof rebels assuming the attitude they did was,
that Sandilli was moving this way with the intention of taking possession
of these fastnesses, when they would join him, and that the farm servants
were then to rise and make a raid on their masters, carrying off their stock
into these fastnesses for the maintenance of Sandilli and his warriors. I
therefore decided to lose no more time, but to strike a blow which would
not only smash up these rebels, but which would also strike terror into
the disaffected farm servants, and also check Sandilli.

On the 15th, before commencing further operations, we sent all the
forces to scour the Schelmkloof, Sweetnam's kloof, and adjoining kloofs, to
see whether they were clear ; not a rebel was to be found.

That afternoon Colonel Palmer and I prepared our plans, and issued
the necessary instructions for the attack on the Waterkloof on the following
day. After dark, and in a very heavy rain, we started off the burghers,
volunteers, and a company of infantry, to take up a position at the western
side of Iron Mountain in the Waterkloof, and to be in positions round west
and north-west at 4 o'clock on the following morning.

At 3 o'clock on the morning of the 16th, two guns and European
infantry were sent to take up positions along the eastern ridges. At the
same hour Colonel Palmer and I, with the main column with two guns,
went down the 12th Pass to take up position along the south and south-
east, placing volunteers and infantry to cut off retreat into either Arries'
hoek or Schelmkloof. The burghers under Bowker and Campbell were
first in position. The rebels opened fire upon the burghers. But the
rebels were very soon overpowered, several of them being killed, and a
large number of cattle captured. The rebels became terror-stricken, and
fled to the Iron Mountain and adjacent kloofs ; they raised the war-cry, but
no response was given.

The artillery, under Captain Stuart Smith, and his officers, on this
occasion, did splendid service with their guns, in shelling the kloofs, and
in cutting off the cattle from the rebels. The infantry also did well in
searching the kloofs with volleys of musketry ; and in short the whole of
our forces worked well.

On the previous evening these rebels had attacked a farmer named
Klopper, and carried off his cattle ; we succeeded in recovering them on the

morning of the 16th, several of the rebels who made that attack having been shot in the engagement that morning.

We had all a very severe march back to Fort Fordyce, on account of very heavy thunderstorms that afternoon.

The 17th being Sunday, and all very tired, we remained in camp.

On the 18th the infantry with two guns, burghers, and native levies, started at 3 o'clock a.m., and again went through the Waterkloof.

The burghers came upon the rebels at a cave near the Iron Mountain. The rebels made a determined stand, but Bowker's Rovers soon overpowered them, killing 14, and driving the remainder out of the fastness.

A large number of women and children were found and brought out. Amongst them was Tini Macomo's wife, who informed us that her husband and his brother had a very narrow escape, and that they, with four or five followers, had bolted when they found our forces getting the better of them. The Waterkloof, Iron Mountain, and surrounding kloofs were well searched. All the cattle found were captured, and all the women and children sent to Fort Beaufort.

We kept up constant patrols throughout the Waterkloof and Schelmkloof up to the 27th March, and satisfied ourselves that the country was clear.

I myself, with 50 mounted men, went down the Waterkloof, over Bush Neck, thence to the Koonap, across to the Mancazana, up Doornkloof to Oliphant's Bush, crossed the mountains back to Mancazana to Bennett's, thence to the foot of Winterberg round to Kaal Hoek, and so on back to Fordyce.

I found the farmers all highly delighted at our operations in Schelmkloof and Waterkloof; they stated that we did not take possession of these Kafir strongholds a day too soon; that their servants had all been very restless and insolent; that it had been Sandilli's intention to come and take possession of these fastnesses, and that the servants were to have carried off their masters' stock as a commissariat for Sandilli, whom they were to join in these fastnesses; but that our determined and successful operations had struck terror into the natives, who had settled down quietly, and were altogether changed for the better. The farmers stated they now felt a security they had not experienced for many years.

Such of the Kafirs as I thought it advisable to disarm, gave up their arms willingly, and many of them voluntarily gave up their arms, to their masters, and many farmers who had deserted their farms, in consequence of the unsatisfactory state of affairs, were now returning to their farms.

I have much pleasure in reporting that we won these fastnesses without any casualty on our side.

Our forces all worked well, harmoniously and cheerfully, and Colonel Palmer will bring their services to the notice of the Government.

I shall be glad if reference will be made to the sketch furnished to His Excellency the Commander of the Forces by Lieutenant Cameron, Royal Engineer, and accompanying Colonel Palmer's report.

To keep possession of these fastnesses we have established posts as follows:

Round Schelmkloof.

At Snodgrass's, 50 soldiers and 15 Native Police; at Sweetnam's, 45 Balfour volunteers; at Cross's, 30 soldiers and 15 Native Police; at Bennett's, 10 Native Police; at Hartley's, 10 Native Police; At Fort Fordyce, and commanding both Schelmkloof and Waterkloof, 60 soldiers, 2 guns and 25 Native Police.

Round Waterkloof.

At Botha's farm, a company of soldiers and 15 Native Police; at

Botha's Vee Kraal, 50 Hottentot Militia ; at Moss's farm, 24 Native Police and 40 of Pope's Levies ; at Vice's, commanding Kroome range, 30 soldiers and 10 Native Police.

Bowker with 50 of his burghers to patrol the country from Moordenaar's kloof to Maasdorp forest, and watch any movements of Sandilli.

I have ascertained from reliable native sources that after his narrow escape on the 18th, Tini Macomo and his brother, with 10 followers cleared out of this altogether, and went towards Sandilli.

His women also informed me that prior to our operations he had sent five messengers to Sandilli, requesting Sandilli to send him assistance, but that these messengers never returned.

On the 27th March Colonel Palmer and I, with the remainder of the forces, left Fort Fordyce for Fort Beaufort. We travelled *via* Buxton, Balfour, &c.; I myself going on to Seymour.

I found the farmers all greatly rejoiced at our operations ; many of them who had been in laager for months in consequence of the hostile attitude of the Schelmkloof and Waterkloof Kafirs, had since our operations at these places broken up their laagers and returned to their farms ; they had also commenced ploughing, and one and all throughout the whole of the surrounding country are unanimous in saying that we did not take possession of these fastnesses a day too soon.

All spoke with the greatest satisfaction of the good which our operations had done to the natives.

Mr. Borcherds will of course himself report to the Government on the natives in his district, their giving up their arms, and their requesting to be registered as loyal.

Our tour through that part of the country did a great deal of good ; it inspired confidence to all.

I spoke kindly to the Kafirs, and pointed out to them the disastrous results of disloyalty, and advised them to live an honest, industrious, and loyal life.

We arrived at Fort Beaufort on the 30th March.

In making this report, I have to request that my telegrams to the Government may be taken as part and parcel of it.

In an expedition of this kind with so many undisciplined forces, cases of hardship and injustice must occur, where the innocent have been made to suffer with the guilty.

Such cases have occurred, and I am only astonished there has not been more of them, but from the very first, and throughout the whole of our operations, Colonel Palmer and I have set our faces against any unjust act.

We have dealt severely with any of our men whom we have found committing any dishonest or unjust act.

Some Fingoes from Heald Town and other places who went out on their own account, and carried off cattle belonging to Kafirs who ought not to have been interfered with, have by our orders been apprehended and sent to gaol, and are to be tried for theft, and the cattle have been restored to the owners.

Cases of hardship have occurred owing to the actions of some of our men, but Colonel Palmer and I have given a willing ear to every complaint, and some of such cases we have already settled to the satisfaction of the complainants, and others are still receiving our attention, and I have every hope that they also will be satisfactorily settled.

I beg to impress upon the Government the necessity of keeping this place well garrisoned, and of sending some Frontier Armed Mounted Police to occupy the posts we have established and to keep up a constant patrolling.

I also recommend strongly that a fair valuation be made of that country, and that Government should purchase it from the present private proprietors, and then parcel it out into small lots and grant it on very easy terms to, say, German immigrants, with strict prohibitive conditions regarding Kafirs being allowed again to occupy it.

We have now won these fastnesses, and are in possession of them, and we should never again allow them to fall into the hands of the natives.

Allowing Kafirs to squat on their farms, and taking them on as tenants, has been the curse and ruin of the farmers in this part of the country ; the Kafirs have only been robbing the farmers to pay their rents, and they have led an idle and lawless life.

The farmers were obliged to leave their farms, and farming was coming to a standstill ; the country was gradually falling into the hands of the Kafirs, and they nearly gained possession of these terrible and favourite strongholds of the Gaikas, the Schelmkloof and Waterkloof.

It has cost the country a good sum to remedy these evils, and a law should therefore be enacted to prevent a recurrence of such evils.

In conclusion, I beg to bring to the notice of the Government the harmonious manner in which the Imperial and Colonial Forces worked together ; no unpleasantness of any kind occurred throughout the whole of the expedition, and all worked in a most rugged country, and under the greatest hardships, with a cheerfulness and willingness which deserve every praise.

About two thousand head of cattle, five hundred sheep and goats, and fifty horses, were captured, these are to be sold, and the proceeds paid into the bank.

Some impartial person will afterwards be appointed to divide these proceeds among the forces which were engaged.

Colonel Palmer has forwarded from time to time full and detailed reports of the work performed by the forces under his command, and I would suggest that you request His Excellency the Commander of the Forces to allow you to peruse these reports, and to examine the sketches accompanying them.

It has been a source of great satisfaction to me to be associated with Colonel Palmer in this matter ; he has rendered me every assistance, and we have worked most harmoniously together, and as a representative of the Civil Government, I take this opportunity of thanking Colonel Palmer, the officers of his regiment, the officer of the 24th Regiment, Lieutenant Cameron of the Royal Engineers, and Captain Stuart Smith and Lieutenants Curling and Fowler of the Royal Artillery, for their kindness towards me, during the whole of this expedition, and for the valuable assistance they have rendered me, and also to acknowledge the excellent manner in which the Commissariat Officers under the greatest difficulties have discharged their duties.

To the Colonial Forces and their officers my best thanks are due, and I feel sure that Colonel Palmer will bring their valuable services to the notice of the Government, so that it is unnecessary for me to particularize them here.

Having done all that I have considered necessary to carry out the wishes of the Government, I shall now return to my duties at Cradock, trusting that my actions will meet with your approval.

I have &c.,

(Signed)   W. B. CHALMERS,
            Special Commissioner.

POSITION OF THE IMPERIAL AND COLONIAL FORCES ON THE MORNING OF THE
5TH MARCH, 1878.

1. The main body of the 90th Light Infantry, one company of the
24th Regiment, and two guns, Royal Artrillery, were concentrated at
Blinkwater on the night of the 4th March; they then proceeded to Snodgrass's farm, where they were joined by the Stockenstrom Rifle Volunteers
under Captain Green, the Stockenstrom Militia under Captain Smit, 50 of
Mr. Blakeway's District Native Police, 50 of Captain Pope's Fingo Levy,
and 26 of the Beaufort Rangers (volunteers) under Captain Richards, all
were in position by 3 a.m. on the 5th March.

2. 20 men of the Beaufort Rangers took up a position on the road
between Hard's Farm and Fuller's Hoek, by 3 a.m. on the 5th March.

3. The Stockenstrom Volunteer Cavalry, under Lieutenant Elliott, 30
men of the District Native Police; all under command of Sub-Inspector
Atmore, took up a position by 3 a.m. on the 5th March, as follows, viz:
from the outspan on the top of the Blinkwater Hill, through Cross's Farm,
extending to Mordenaar's Kloof.

4. 2 guns Royal Artillery, 80 men 90th Light Infantry, marched to
Deel Kraal, and from thence to the springs, and from there marched to
reach Shawe's Native School by 3 a.m. on the 5th March; the Winterberg Grey's Volunteers under Captain Sweetnam accompanied this column
from Deel Kraal. The whole to protect the position in front of Shawe's
Native School house (facing the Schelmkloof), and to their left as far as
the Blinkwater Hill Road, and also to communicate with the burgher
force patrols on their right. Captain Swetnam should patrol from Shawe's
Native School, not only as far as the top of the Blinkwater Hill, but so
far beyond as may be necessary, so as to communicate with the right of
the force under Sub-Inspector Atmore.

5. The burgher force at Fort Fordyce, consisting of the following
corps, viz, The Adelaide Volunteer Cavalry under Captain Holland,
Bowker's Burghers under Captain Bowker, Post Retief Burghers under
Captain Edwards, Winterberg Burghers, under Field-cornet Viljoen,
Kraal Hoek Burghers, under Captain Dreyer, the whole under command of
Commandant P. Campbell, were to be in position by 3 a.m. on the 5th
March, and to extend from Fort Fordyce to their left until they communi-
cated with the right of the party at Shawe's Native School House, also to
patrol the open ground between the Schelmkloof and Fuller's Hoek, and
down the Argyle Road to Campbell's Beacon, about 3 miles from Fort
Fordyce.

6. 100 of the Fingo levy under Captain Pope, 60 of the District
Native Police under Sub-Inspector W. G. Campbell, the whole under command of Mr. Booth, were to be in position by 3 a.m. on the 15th March, as
follows. To occupy the velt of bush in front of the Fingo location,
extending to the rear of the Kafir location occupied by Tini Macomo.

(Signed)   J. H. LAYE,
Captain 90th Light Infantry, Staff Officer,

2nd April, 1878.

[B.]

TO THE KAFIRS IN WATERKLOOF, &c.

1. The Government does not wish to shoot you down, or seize your
cattle if you submit to the orders of the Government.

2. On account of the great trouble which the Kafirs in Schelmkloof and Waterkloof have given for a long time past, the Government is determined that these fastnesses shall no longer be occupied by Kafirs.

3. The Kafirs in the Blinkwater, Sweetnam's Kloof and Schelmkloof refused to move out quietly, the consequence to them therefore have been most disastrous.

4. If you, the Kafirs in the Waterkloof and Iron Mountain, will submit and come to me and give up all your guns and assegais, and leave these fastnesses quietly, you will not be interfered with. I shall give you passes to remove with your cattle, women and children, either to service in the colony, or to Kama's, Toi's, or Siwani's locations.

5. I give you up till mid-day to-morrow to comply with this demand of the Government.

6. Send your answer by Philip who carries this; and if these two men do not return with an answer from you by mid-day to-morrow, I shall look upon it as a refusal on your part to comply with this demand.

(Signed)   W. B. CHALMERS
Civil Commissioner of Cradock,
Special Commissioner Fort Fordyce.

14th March. 1878.

Fort Beaufort April 3rd, 1878.

MY DEAR MR. AYLIFF,—I send herewith the correspondence on the case of Chete, my teacher, and Hans, &c., upon which I do not need to make further remark.

My conviction is that it was needful to have the Gaika Kafirs cleared out of the Waterkloof; whether it has been done in the right or best manner is another question, as my case was not connected with the Waterkloof at all.

I did not write to congratulate you on your promotion to your present honourable and responsible position, as we had talked about it before, and you knew my sentiments upon it.

I have great relief and satisfaction in the removal of the Molteno ministry and the installation of the present ministry. I truly and heartily desire that they may succeed and secure such a majority in the Assembly as will enable them to carry on the Government with vigour and satisfaction.

Mr. Sprigg has been greatly lionized in Graham's Town, and has expressed his views very fully and freely.

It is more than a quarter of a century ago since, when I published my History of Natal, I advocated the policy now so clearly and strongly set forth by Mr. Sprigg and yourself. See History of Natal, "Government of Natives," p.p. 182, &c., &c.

This policy I have advocated ever since; had it been acted upon there would have been no Langalabalele affair, and had not Mr. Shepstone altered his views and practice, he could not have become what he now is.

I shall watch with a good deal of interest the course of events for the next few months. I shall do more, I shall pray that the God of nations may guide our Governor and his advisers aright.

I was greatly pleased with the courteous manner of the Governor in my interview with him.

I am, &c.,
(Signed)   W. C. HOLDEN.

P.S.—Since the above was written you will see that I have added the last part of the correspondence. You have now the whole case before you.

(Signed)   W. C. HOLDEN.

Fort Beaufort, 3rd April, 1878.

FROM LIEUTENANT-COLONEL H. W. PALMER, 90TH LIGHT INFANTRY, COMMANDING THE TROOPS, FORT BEAUFORT DISTRICT, TO THE HONOURABLE THE SECRETARY FOR NATIVE AFFAIRS, KING WILLIAM'S TOWN.

SIR,—I have the honour to report, in reply to your telegram of this day's date, that I entirely concur with Mr. Chalmers, the Special Commissioner, not to allow the country, known as the Schelmkloof and Waterkloof, and its vicinity, to be re-occupied by Kafirs. It is one full of fastnesses and strongholds, they are always sure to avail themselves of, in the event of any difficulty or trouble with them ; it is now thoroughly clear of them, to all intents and purposes, and a difficult job it was to get them out of it.

I have surrounded and occupied it by posts, who are now patrolling in all directions thereabouts to prevent its re-occupation, and these outposts should be maintained, if that part of the country is to be kept clear of Kafirs, until it is otherwise allotted, and disposed of by Government.

I have sent two companies of the 90th Light Infantry to Fort Cox and Burn's Hill this morning, and now not a complete company of the corps left here ; but I am fully occupied in looking after and provisioning my various outposts in this district.

The whole of the farmers from all over these parts have signed an address to myself and Mr. Chalmers, an expression of their thanks for our recent operations in removing a scourge (as they term it) from which they have long suffered ; and express their gratitude to the present Government and ministry for having adopted such vigorous action, as the only way to ensure success, and wish the Fish River Bush and other adjacent notorious locations to be similarly dealt with.

I have, &c.,

(Signed)   H. W. PALMER,
Lieutenant-Colonel 90th Light Infantry,
Commanding the Troops, Fort Beaufort District.

EXTRACT FROM THE "ARGUS," 4th APRIL, 1878.

There is another case of outrageous hardship, to which we invite our readers' attention.

A farmer, named Hards, had a farm adjoining Tini Macomo's, but when the operations against the latter commenced, he went away, leaving his cattle and ostriches in charge of his native servants. Sweetnam's volunteers, with some troops, appeared on the farm, and overflowing with military ardour, began to "operate" on the huts and cattle of Mr. Hard's servants.

The huts were burnt, the cattle seized, and the servants and their families made prisoners. Mr. Hard's own cattle were subsequently driven out of their enclosure, and made booty of, so that the farm was completely cleared of servants and stock, and Mr. Hards reduced to beggary. The poor man is informed that he can get no redress unless he makes a pilgrimage to Cape Town, an undertaking that it is just possible, under the circumstances, he may not be equal to.

Richard Edward Hards, being duly sworn, states :—I am a farmer residing at Argyle, Blinkwater. It adjoins the farm lately occupied by Tini Macomo. I had 12 Kafirs in my employ. I left my farm three days after the expedition went out. Some days after this, whilst in Fort Beaufort, one of my servants came and informed me that my cattle had been taken by the troops. I reported the matter by letter to the Civil Commissioner ; two days after I received an answer that the cattle had been returned the same day, and this I found on inquiry was the case.

Some cattle belonging to my servants were not taken at all ; those that were taken were forwarded to Fort Beaufort, the same day they arrived the Resident Magistrate investigated the matter, and ordered the cattle to be restored to my servants, after fully enquiring into each case separately. Eight huts belodging to my Kafir servants were burnt ; the loss of these, and of the time my servants were detained at Fort Beaufort and at the farm, and of the use of my oxen, are the only losses I have sustained. I have never been told by anyone that I must go to Cape Town if I wanted redress.

I, Ben Herbert Holland, solemnly and sincerely declare that the foregoing statement was made to me by Mr. Hards, and when read over to him he stated it was correct, but refused to attach his signature to it.

(Signed)   B. H. HOLLAND,
Resident Magistrate and Civil Commissioner,
Fort Beaufort.

Declared before me at Fort Beaufort this 18th April, 1878.

(Signed)   JOHN HARVEY,
Justice of the Peace.

Fort Beaufort, 5th April, 1878.

FROM LIEUTENANT-COLONEL H. W. PALMER, 90TH LIGHT INFANTRY, COMMANDING THE TROOPS, FORT BEAUFORT DISTRICT, TO B. H. HOLLAND ESQ, CIVIL COMMISSIONER AND RESIDENT MAGISTRATE, FORT BEAUFORT.

SIR,—I have the honour to return the copy of the telegram that accompanied your letter of this day's date, and at the same time to transmit a copy in English of Mr. Chalmers's manifesto, which he addressed in Kafir to the rebels in the Waterkloof, and beg to add that for three days previously, he was verbally communicating with them, through messengers, to the same effect without any satisfactory result. I am receiving daily reports from the various posts surrounding the Schelmkloof and Waterkloof, who are constantly patrolling both by day and night, so that Mr. Blakeway's doing so at present would seem not to be necessary. I shall however, convey your message to him.

I have already reported to the Secretary for Native Affairs that in my opinion no Kafir should be permitted to re-occupy the ground from which we have removed them.

I have, &c.,

(Signed)   H. W. PALMER,
Lieutenant-Colonel 90th Light Infantry
Commanding the Troops Fort Beaufort District.

Civil Commissioner's Office,
Fort Beaufort, 5th April, 1878.

The Honourable the Secretary for Native Affairs,
King William's Town.

Sir,—In compliance with your telegram of the 5th instant, I have the honour to enclose copy of Mr. Chalmers's manifesto, calling upon all loyal natives to come out of Waterkloof.

I also enclose copy of a letter received from Colonel Palmer, having reference to the same matter.

I have, &c.,

(Signed)   B. H. HOLLAND,
Civil Commissioner.

Commandant-General.   Referred.
(Signed)   G. W. PATON, Captain,
Colonial Military Secretary.
9th April, 1878.

The Honourable the Secretary
for Native Affairs, King
William's Town.

Will you be good enough to give me authority to call upon burghers and volunteers to turn out and occupy the posts in the Waterkloof, from which the general wishes to withdraw the regular troops.

CHARLES D. GRIFFITH,
Commandant-General.
King William's Town,
9th April, 1878.

King William's Town,
9th April, 1878.
Colonial Military Secretary.

Operations in the Waterkloof being over, and it being understood that Mr. Chalmers was able to arrange for the Colonial Forces on the spot taking up the most important posts, and so relieving Her Majesty's troops for services elsewhere,—orders have been sent to Lieutenant-Colonel Palmer to proceed with two companies of the 90th Regiment and two guns, Royal Artillery, to occupy Fort Hare,—and for the remaining two guns, Royal Artillery, to be sent to King William's Town. This will still leave one company of the 90th Regiment at Fort Beaufort.

It is requested that instructions may be sent by telegraph to the Civil Commissioner to facilitate the immediate relief of the troops under orders for Fort Hare, their presence being urgently required in the Alice District.

By order,
(Signed)   W. BELLAIRS.
District Adjutant-General.

Civil Commissioner's Office, Fort Beaufort,
11th April, 1878.

The Under Colonial Secretary, Cape Town.

Sir,—I have the honour to enclose, for the consideration of Government, copy of a letter from Colonel Palmer, commanding the troops in this district, giving cover to one from the Rev. Mr. Holden, claiming compensation on behalf of "Chete," "Hans," and "Klaas," for property destroyed and cattle taken from them by certain of the forces employed in the late expedition against Tini Macomo and others.

I referred the matter for report to Mr. Booth, the inspector of the location where these people resided, and beg to annex a copy of the same.

With reference to the claims of Hans and Klaas, it will be seen that by the Native Locations Act, No. 6, of 1876, all their stock should have been registered, failing which, according to the 7th and 8th sections, the same would be liable to be impounded and sold, unless they could prove to the satisfaction of the inspector that it was their *bonâ fide* property.

All cattle duly registered appear to have been given up to these men, and as they have not attempted to show how the other animals claimed came into their possession, I consider at present they have failed to make out any case for compensation.

With regard to Chete, the value of his goods appears to have increased considerably within the last few weeks, as will be seen by reference to copy of a letter sent to me by Mr. Holden on the 14th March, wherein he only claims £10 or £12, for loss of books, clothes, &c., and makes no claim for loss of crops. The cost price of the saddle was then put down at £6, he now claims £6 10s. for it.

Taking everything into consideration I would suggest that Chete be allowed £15, which amount I feel convinced will more than cover all his losses, the wardrobe and library of a man in his position not usually being very extensive, and I have every reason to believe his crops, if he ever possessed any, must have been a failure on account of the severity of the drought in that part.

I would beg to draw the attention of Government to the manner in which Chete has been in the habit of conducting this so-called school : from what Mr. Booth says, it would appear that he is certainly not deserving of any future support from Government as a teacher. I think if the truth were known he has been imposing on the credulity of Mr. Holden for some time past.

I have, &c.,

(Signed)   B. H. HOLLAND,
Civil Commissioner.

Fort Beaufort, 4th April, 1878.

To B. H. Holland Esq., Civil Commissioner, and Resident Magistrate,
Fort Beaufort.

SIR,—In the absence of Mr. Chalmers, I think it best to submit to you the attached correspondence, for your opinion and legal investigation, pending which I shall not say what I think of it.

In the event of your finding any difficulty in dealing with it, I suggest your forwarding it to Mr. Chalmers, asking him to report to Government, if he thinks such a course necessary regarding this matter. You will see from this attached envelope, that Mr. Holden's communication was meant for either Mr. Chalmers or myself.

I have, &c.,

(Signed)   H. W. PALMER,
Lieutenant-Colonel 90th Light Infantry,
Commanding the Troops Fort Beaufort District.

REPORT ON THE CLAIMS OF HANS AND KLAAS.

Hans, a tenant on the farm of St. Lawrence. I registered his stock on the 26th January, 1877, as follows : 14 oxen, 14 cows, 2 bulls, 1 heifer, 13 calves ; in all 44 head ; 1 horse, 125 sheep, 3 goats.

I inspected on the 18th May, 1877, stock as follows : 17 oxen, 12 cows, 2 bulls, one heifer, 11 calves ; in all 43, 64 sheep, 3 goats.

I again inspected on the 30th October, 1877, 13 oxen, 10 cows, 1 bull, 1 heifer, 11 calves ; in all 36 ; 14 sheep, 1 goat. Hans has removed to Mount Pleasant, Mr. Shaw's farm.

Mr. Chalmers gave an order to Mr. Edwards for the above number of cattle, 36 head, and Hans has no claim for any greater number. I don't understand Mr. Holden's statement, that I refused to register Hans' claim ; this is not correct.

"Klass" received an order for the number of cattle he stated he had, and having the book with me at Fort Fordyce, in which his cattle were registered, the statement that I refused to register his claims is also incorrect.

I believe the huts (not horses) of both "Hans" and "Klaas" were burnt, but this was necessary to prevent them being occupied by rebels.

Hans has got his wagon, as well as one belonging to Donker, who formerly resided at Mount Pleasant (but not at Middeldrift).

I hear from Mr. Hartley that Hans and Klaas are quarrelling about who shall have it.

(Signed)   B. BOOTH,
Inspector of Native Locations.

REPORT ON "CHETE'S" SCHOOL AND CLAIMS.

The first time I met "Chete" was on the farm of St. Lawrence, early in the morning of the 26th January, 1877. I asked him who he was ; he said, "I am the schoolmaster on Mr. Shaw's farm, and I lodge here." I told him I had been three or four times at the school house, and always found it closed. He replied it was holiday time. I enquired how many scholars he had ; his reply was seven, the people do not care to send their children to school.

The second and last time I met him was near the hut of Xamba on "Allemans Fontein;" he said he lodged with Xamba. I again told him that I had been at his school the previous three days, and found it closed.

I asked as to the average attendance ; his reply was about seven. He told me that the Inspector of Schools had been up, and that they had a muster of 35 scholars.

I asked if he was aware of the inspector's visit ; he said yes, some days previous to his coming. I said then, "That accounts for the large number on that day."

During last year I passed the school house more than a dozen times, and always found it closed. I have never been inside the school house, therefore have never had an opportunity of judging the value of "Chete's" property. From what I have above stated, and which two or three parties will confirm, "Chete" has very little claim on the parents of the children for school fees.

I don't know the locality of "Chete's" mealie lands, so can give no information as to the largeness of the acres, or their probable yield, but, judging from the appearance of the mealie lands in that part, the yield would be very small.

(Signed)   B. BOOTH,
Inspector of Native Locations.

FROM CIVIL COMMISSIONER, FORT BEAUFORT, TO SECRETARY FOR NATIVE
AFFAIRS, KING WILLIAM'S TOWN.

Colonel Palmer has shown me a telegram from Deputy Adjutant
General, that the European troops on outpost surrounding Water and
Schelm Kloofs, are to be relieved by colonial troops. He has at present
two hundred and fifty men at different stations, and I have only one
hundred and thirty of Pope's Fingoes available to replace, leaving this
place without any native forces.

Colonel Palmer and Chalmers both agreed that the posts established
by them are absolutely requisite to keep Waterkloof and Schelmkloof free
from Kafirs, in which I concur. I think it should be left to Colonel Palmer
to detach such forces as he can spare without interfering with the necessary arrangements that have been made for the occupation of very important points. I think it is a pity to remove the guns from Fort Fordyce at
present, but presume Colonel Palmer must carry out his instructions.

9th April, 1878.

Telegrams.

FROM CIVIL COMMISSIONER, FORT BEAUFORT, TO SECRETARY FOR NATIVE
AFFAIRS, KING WILLIAM'S TOWN.

Colonel Palmer of opinion, in addition to company 90th at Fordyce,
absolutely necessary to have few regulars at top of Blinkwater Hill. I
quite agree, and consider it a great mistake to have this important district
without artillery. Colonel Palmer wanted 30 mounted men stationed at
Koonap Post. Can I engage the services of thirty burghers or volunteers
for purpose, and enrol them for three months for service there or elsewhere
if required, on usual terms?

13th April, 1878.

FROM CIVIL COMMISSIONER, FORT BEAUFORT, TO SECRETARY FOR NATIVE
AFFAIRS, KING WILLIAM'S TOWN.

Had already acted on your first telegram, authorizing balance of
clothing to Bowker's men, when I received my second to-night.

Think it will be unwise to shift his men from their present importan
stations.

Could get twenty mounted volunteers to do duty, at Koonap Post, at
ten shillings a day, to cover everything, pay, rations, and forage.

Will you authorize me?

13th April, 1878.

Civil Commissioner's Office,
Fort Beaufort, 22nd April, 1878.

The Honourable the Colonial Secretary, King William's Town.

SIR,—Notwithstanding the approval of Government, expressed by
yourself both to Mr. Chalmers and Colonel Palmer, as to the satisfactory
manner in which the Waterkloof and Schelmkloof expedition was carried

out, it has never been noticed in general orders, at which the forces engaged in these operations feel sore ; this apparent oversight, I presume, is owing to the fact that the expedition was undertaken during the time that Sir Arthur Cunynghame was in command of the forces, and was concluded shortly after the arrival of General Thesiger.

One word from you would, no doubt, remedy the omission, and all concerned would be gratified by some notice in general orders, and thus regulars, burghers, and levies would be encouraged in future operations.

I have, &c.,

(Signed)   B. H. HOLLAND,
Civil Commissioner.

Fort Beaufort, April 9th, 1878.

His Honour William Ayliff, Esq., Secretary of Native Affairs,
Cape Colony.

Sir,—I have the honour to forward a copy of the whole correspondence which has passed between myself and Colonel Palmer, Special Commissioner Chalmers, and the magistrate of Fort Beaufort, on the subject of Hans, Chete and others. The former part of this correspondence I was sending a week ago, as the latter part will explain. As nearly a week has passed since my last letter to Colonel Palmer, and I have received no answer, I now forward the whole to your Honour with only this addition to what I wrote in my last to you on the 2nd instant.

The *Graham's Town Journal* of the 5th instant, has the following,— "It is said that the booty of the Tarkastad volunteers has realized £4,611 ; they were forty-three days absent."

The captain of these volunteers was Mr. Mundle, as stated in this correspondence ; who with his men seized the cattle and persons of three innocent victims.

I do not allow myself to comment upon these disgraceful transactions, but trust that Government will speedily adopt such methods as may meet the case of the innocent and oppressed, and at the same time eradicate its own honour.

I have, &c.,

(Signed)   W. CLIFFORD HOLDEN, W.M.

Referred to the Resident Magistrate of Fort Beaufort for report.

(Signed)   WILLIAM AYLIFF,
Secretary for Native Affairs.

Office of Secretary for Native Affairs,
King William's Town, 17th April, 1878.

Have already reported fully on this matter, *vide* my letter to Colonial Secretary, dated 11th April, 1878.

Mr. Holden is mistaken in saying that the cattle taken by Tarkastad vclunteers realized £4,611 ; the stock taken by the whole force has not yet realized more than half that amount.

(Signed)   B. H. HOLLAND,
Civil Commissioner.

Civil Commissioner's Office,
    Fort Beaufort, 23rd April, 1878.

Waterkloof Expedition.

With reference to the article in the *Cape Argus* about the expedition to the Waterkloof and Schelmkloof, we are sure the subjoined letter from Government to the Special Commissioner will speak for itself :—

Copy.]

Colonial Secretary's Office,
Cape Town, 17th April, 1878.

SIR,—I have the honour to acknowledge the receipt of your letter, dated the 10th instant, pointing out the inaccuracy of certain remarks made in the *Cape Argus* of the 6th instant, upon communications addressed to you by the Civil Commissioner, Fort Beaufort, on the subject of the Waterkloof expedition against Tini Macomo ; and requesting that your letter now under acknowledgment may be published in refutation of the misstatements contained in the article referred to.

In reply, I am directed to inform you that the Government is perfectly satisfied with your conduct of the difficult duty assigned to you in connexion with the expedition, and considers that with that assurance before you, no appeal to the public through newspapers is either desirable or necessary.

I have, &c.,
(Signed)   CHARLES MILLS,
Under Colonial Secretary.

Alice Times, April 26th.

My diary at Fort Fordyce. We made a start again about 2 o'clock, as we had some distance to travel, our object being to surround Tini Macomo's kraal at daybreak. It was still raining.

Tuesday, 5th—We travelled as usual with every precaution and as quietly as possible, so as not to alarm the Kafirs. I omitted to mention that Lieutenant Solomon started in another direction from Blinkwater so as to meet us at the kraal. Having reached the drift, which is about 500 yards from Tini's kraal, we halted and waited for daybreak. The soldiers meanwhile were held in reserve at about half a mile from us, it being arranged that the rangers under Captain Richards make the attack supported by the Fingoes. Just as day broke, the word "forward" was given, and off we went at full galop ; when 150 yards of the huts the Kafirs rushed out in all directions with their guns and assegais, making for the bush. "Halt," "halt!" and all other persuasions possible for them to stop, but to no avail.

The order was then given to fire upon them as they were escaping with their guns and assegais into the bush. Upon this Captain Richards dismounted and fired, the ball striking at one of the Kafir's feet. He stood dead still and surrendered himself to us with a bundle of assegais. A bullet whizzing just over my head made me turn round, and seeing two Kafirs just entering the bush I fired, but to what effect I don't know. Another Kafir was just aiming at Trooper Tidbury, when a well directed ball from his rifle, just in time, laid the Kafir low. Two more Kafirs jumped out of a hut close to me and were making for the bush. Captain Blakeway of the Fingoes and myself rushed up to them, took one of them prisoners and disarmed him, the other made his escape.

Firing was now going on all around Fuller's Hoek ; the bullets flying over our heads. The Kafirs now raised the war cry and out they came from all directions shouting from hill to hill. The hill about 1,000 yards away from us appeared red with Kafirs who were making for the bush with their guns and assegais. We being too few in numbers, could not think of attacking so large a body of Kafirs. Lieutenant Solomon with the other division of Rangers did not come up in time. We had only six Fingoes, under Lieutenant Ward, with us. The Kafirs dared us to go any further, and fired upon us. Upon this we opened fire upon them, advancing at the same time.

The reinforcements we had been anxiously expecting came up. This soon made the Kafirs clear. During the interval we were waiting for reinforcements the Rangers captured 200 head of cattle and sheep. All the huts were now being burnt. As we halted before the ridge of the hill a Kafir boldly stepped out of the bush, concealed himself behind a tree, and let fly at us, the bullet falling about 20 yards in front of the soldiers. Several shots were fired at him, but he escaped. We now proceeded up the kloof, but could not get further than Snodgrass's farm, which was occupied by the Balfour Volunteers. Owing to the rain and the bad state of the roads, we had to return to the outside of the kloof, and as the wagons came up we pitched camp, the soldiers also pitching their tents. Here we had to remain the whole day as it was raining. Several of the captured oxen were killed for rations : in all we took over 200 head of cattle, a few sheep and goats, and 28 prisoners ; the loss of the enemy was two killed.

Wednesday 6th.—Still raining, report just come down that the Balfour Volunteers stationed at Snodgrass's farm, seeing a number of cattle higher up the kloof, went up to capture them when the Kafirs turned out, the Volunteers seeing the force too strong for them returned.—8 p.m. Express just in from Captain Stevens, who is in command of the forces at Fort Fordyce, that Kafirs were in great force in Sweetnam's kloof. Thursday 7th.—Beautiful clear sky. At 4 a.m. we commenced to prepare for a move to commence operations according to order. Being ready, off we started at 6 a.m., the Rangers being in the advance as usual. At the start one of the officers proposed to separate the Rangers in two divisions, but the colonel would not. At first bushy kloof, the Fingo and Hottentot levies were ordered in to scour it ; they no sooner entered than they were fired upon by the Kafirs.

Civil Commissioner's Office, Fort Beaufort,

30th April, 1878.

The Under Colonial Secretary, Cape Town.

SIR,—With reference to my report of the 11th instant, upon certain claims made by the Reverend W. Holden on behalf of "Chete," "Hans," and "Klaas," I beg to enclose copies of two depositions taken before me this morning, which throw some light on the character of these men.

I have, &c.,

(Signed)   B. H. HOLLAND.

Civil Commissioner.

At Fort Beaufort, 30th April, 1878.

Jantje Jonas, being duly sworn, states :—I am a sergeant in Mr. Booth's police. I remember Van Vener, a farmer, coming to my station at Bush Neck, and reporting the loss of four oxen. I and seven of the police accompanied Van Vener ; we found the spoor of the cattle, and traced it to the ridge at the top of Schelmkloof, near the schoolmaster's house, between the hut and kraal of the headman Suel, a tenant on Mr. Shaw's farm. I called Suel's people, and told them there was a spoor ; they went into their huts and got their arms, consisting of guns and assegais ; there were about 40 of them. I took them to the spot and showed them the spoor. I asked them why they were armed with these guns and assegais ; they said it was their custom.

I said, " You have no Government authority for this." They said there was no Government, there. I said " All right." I then followed the spoor with them. The schoolmaster, " Chete," then joined us. After we had gone a little distance the Kafirs asked me if I was in charge of these policemen. I said," Yes." They said, " Do you know what day it is ?" I replied, " I know it is Sunday." They said, " Look at it for the last time." I advanced towards them and cocked my gun, my men did the same. I said, " *Now* do what you wish." One of the young Kafirs told the others to desist. The schoolmaster then left. I said I wanted the oxen. They then followed the spoor, and I stood still ; they went into the bush which was close to. When the Kafirs showed resistance Mr. Van Vener offered Suel 30s. if he would bring the cattle ; that was why they went into the bush. I said to Mr. Van Vener, " It is not a Government custom to pay thieves to bring out cattle." The five Europeans then rode away ; I and my men remained, and shortly after the oxen were brought out, and they were afterwards handed over to me, and I took them to Van Vener : his farm is 14 miles from where we found the cattle.

I know "Hans ;" he was there, armed with assegais ; I know the schoolmaster lived with him. Hans was there all the time. November and Zenzeba are the only other two I know.

his
(Signed)   JANTJE x JONAS
mark.

Witnesses :

(Signed) B. Booth
    ,,   J. G. Verity.

Before me :

(Signed)   B. H. HOLLAND
Resident Magistrate.

" Muis " and " Tom," being duly sworn, state :—The evidence given by Jantje Jonas, which has just been read over to us, is true and correct in every particular ; we were two of the policemen who accompanied him,

their
(Signed)   MUIS x
TOM x
Witnesses :   marks.

(Signed)   B. Booth
    ,,   J. G. Verity.

Before me :

(Signed)   B. H. HOLLAND,
Resident Magistrate.